es

Teach Their Kids

FREE WORKBOOK

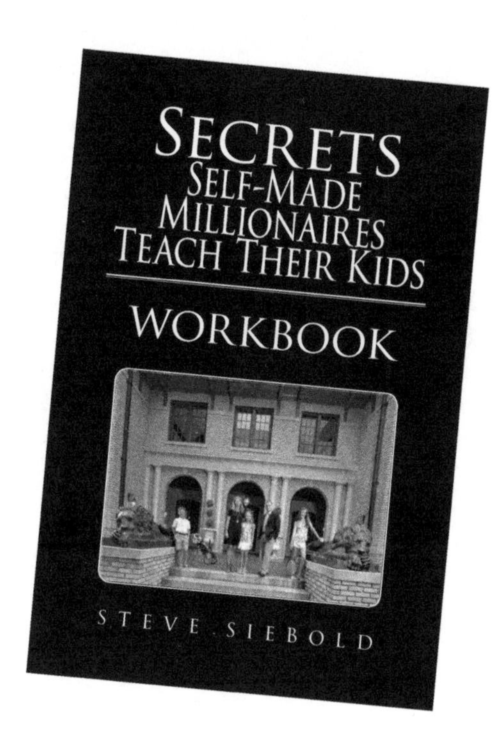

To download FREE workbook please visit:

www.secretsworkbook.com

SECRETS SELF-MADE MILLIONAIRES TEACH THEIR KIDS

STEVE SIEBOLD

Published by London House
www.londonhousepress.com

ISBN-10: 0996516921

Cover Photo by Sam Harris Photography
www.SamHarrisPhotography.com

Back Cover Photo taken from interview with LanBercu TV
www.leadacrosscultures.com

CONTENTS

FOREWORD

by Bo Gibbs

The first time I heard Steve Siebold speak was back in 2006, at our corporate leadership event in Las Vegas. This speech was for our top 2,000 people, regarding the habits, actions and behaviors of great performers. When his first book, 177 Mental Toughness Secrets of the World Class became a bestseller, our field force purchased 20,000 copies. On a personal level, I've used Steve's training to catapult my own wealth advisory practice to the top 1% in the United States.

I'm honored to write the foreword to this book, because I believe it has the power to alter your children's financial future. I believe in these secrets so much, that when Steve asked if I would appear on the cover with my wife and children, I was thrilled. Yes, that's me on the front cover, with my beautiful wife Alison and our three children.

20 years ago, when Alison and I first began our journey together, earning millions of dollars was just a dream. Putting our children in private schools, giving them golf and tennis lessons, and memberships at world-class country clubs, were all mere fantasies. After observing my most successful clients during the early days of my career, when I was struggling to get started, we often wondered what it would be like to raise our kids in a sea of affluence. Now, all of these years later, I see its impact on my own children. The benefits they're reaping are beyond measure.

As a wealth manager specializing in assisting high net worth individuals, I've seen how the self-made rich raise and educate their children. Their examples helped me prepare for my own success, both as a self-made millionaire, and as a parent. That's why this book resonates with me. The secrets Steve writes about are based on his 34-year study of the self-made rich, and while some people may find this content controversial, I've seen these lessons implemented successfully over the past 20 years.

When Siebold states that rich people rule the world, he's not exaggerating. They do. Maybe they shouldn't, but that's the reality. And if you teach your kids exactly how they do it, you'll give them a fighting chance to join this powerful demographic.

The poor may inherit the earth, but the rich *control* it. Again, I'm not suggesting that this is fair. You can either teach your kids how unfair the world is, or you can teach them how to navigate it successfully. The choice is yours. If you chose the latter, this book will be your guide.

Only someone that has been imbedded with the wealthy for over three decades, and conducted 1200+ interviews with the self-made rich, could write this book. The author has devoted his entire adult life to the pursuit of this information, and all you have to do is read and study it with your kids. If you will, you'll be giving them an education they will never get in school. In addition to your love and support, it may be the greatest gift you ever give them.

To your children's future,

Bo Gibbs
Principal
Gibbs Financial Group
Atlanta, Georgia

INTRODUCTION

In 1984, I was a broke college student that wanted to be rich. My college professors seemed more focused on broadening my horizons than my bank account, so I began interviewing self-made millionaires for the answers to financial success. Since then, I've interviewed over 1,200 self-made millionaires and billionaires around the world. One of the key questions I've asked was regarding what they teach their kids about financial success and everything that surrounds it. This book is based on their answers.

The premise of this book is simple: It's success according to the masses vs. success according to self-made millionaires. Like me, you may have been raised and educated with fear-based, scarcity-driven, limited beliefs about wealth and success, but this book guarantees that your kids will learn the opposite.

This book wasn't written for kids, and it wasn't written for adults. It was written *to* kids, with the hope that parents would read it with them. I recommend that you read one secret per day and discuss it with your kids. Each chapter will take 10 minutes or so to complete. In less than 6-months, they will have a better understanding of how and why the rich get richer than most adults.

I wish you the best on your journey into the world of the self-made rich. It's a world only its members have truly understood since the beginning of time… until now.

May your kids become happy and fulfilled self-made millionaires.

Steve Siebold
Bona Allen Mansion
Buford, Georgia
January 1, 2018

CHAPTER 1

Rich People Rule The World

The wealthiest 1% of people own the majority of the world's money, and it's not going to change. This fact is not to be celebrated. To be a member of the world's top 1%, you only need to earn around USD 35,000 per year, and that's due to the staggering number of developing countries and poor people around the world. To be a member of the top 1% in America in 2018, you need to earn around $435,000 per year. Income and wealth disparity is not good for any of the economic classes, including the wealthy. Most rich people are small business owners that need the middle class to purchase their products and services, and when their wages stagnate or drop it has an impact on their profits. The reality is that due to globalization, technology, and other progressive factors, income disparity will continue to grow. It's a more difficult problem to solve than politicians, think tanks and academics would have you believe, and it's not going to happen anytime soon. High school teachers and even college professors may tell you that taxing the rich will solve the problem, but they are wrong, both morally and mathematically. Overtaxing the rich is punishing people for success, and rest assured, they will find a way to stop the government from robbing them. The math shows that stealing from the rich through excessive taxation won't even make a dent in the problem. Be respectful of your teachers, but remember that very few of them are, ever have been, or ever will be, rich.

The best strategy is to join the 1% as quickly as possible and be grateful that you are lucky enough to be born in a country that makes it possible. Also, consider lending a hand to the 99% trying to crack the top 1%.

QUOTE:

"The best way to help the financially struggling is not to become one of them."

ACTION STEP:

Watch the 2013 documentary Inequality for All by former Clinton Administration Labor Secretary Robert Reich.

CRITICAL THINKING QUESTION:

Do you think it's right that rich people rule the world?

MILLIONAIRE RESOURCE:

Read How Rich People Think, by Steve Siebold. This book is based on three decades of interviews with over 1,200 of the wealthiest individuals in the world.

CHAPTER 2

Fall in Love with Work

As a future self-made millionaire, the occupational path you choose to follow will impact every aspect of your life. Since you're going to spend a large percentage of your life working, you want to be sure you love what you're doing. It's difficult to invest the necessary time and energy into a profession that bores you or that has little meaning beyond money. It's wonderful to be rich, but the real windfall is becoming wealthy doing something you would do for free. Waking up everyday with excitement for going to work is a formula for financial abundance, emotional fulfillment, and life satisfaction. This is something only a small percentage of people ever experience, mostly because they fail to plan for it. Piecing together the unique combination of finding work you love, that solves a problem people will pay for, is no easy feat. According to the Gallup Organization, only 13 percent of people enjoy their work. Most people would rather stay at home than go to work. Is it any wonder why so many are broke and unhappy? The masses are not psychologically engaged in what they do for a living, which means they exert minimal effort while demanding maximum compensation. They spend years and small fortunes getting prestigious academic degrees and then enter occupations in which they can't wait to retire. They hate Monday's, thank God for Fridays and live for the weekends, yet they're confounded why they're miserable and broke. This is not the path for you. You've been trained in world-class thinking, and that means finding work you love. This is one of the most important tasks you will ever perform, and it must be done as quickly as possible. Your parents, teachers, and mentors can help, but in the end, you must decide on the work that captures your heart. Only you can make this happen, and today is the day to start thinking about it.

QUOTE:

"If you don't love your work, it's hard to love your life."—Mardy Grothe

ACTION STEP:

Write down ten occupations you would be interested in learning more about.

CRITICAL THINKING QUESTION:

What activity, which you do on a regular basis, makes time go by the fastest?

MILLIONAIRE RESOURCE:

Read: The Amateur: The Pleasures of Doing What You Love, by Andy Merrifield

CHAPTER 3

Success Isn't Free

You're going to hear a lot of lies about financial success from people who've never achieved it. They'll say the rich are evil, shallow, and narcissistic. They'll tell you the wealthy have somehow gamed the system to acquire their fortunes. They'll even claim that the rich just got lucky. Don't believe any of this. To become a self-made millionaire, you're going to have to live and breathe your business 24/7. It's not a task for the faint of heart, the lazy or the entitled. Becoming financially independent will be the fight of your life. You'll have to be willing to sacrifice your time, sleep and leisure to build something great. You'll experience self-doubt; spend endless nights worrying, and you'll come face to face with your deepest fears. It's not glamorous or pretty. While your friends are out having fun, you'll be working, and it will sometimes feel like you're not getting anywhere. You'll be excited in the beginning, but after multiple failures, all you will feel is pain. This is the stage of success that will make or break you. It wears most people down, but if you stay focused on your dream of financial independence, you'll be able to endure. The final stage is the knowing stage, which is when you know you're going to succeed. You may not know how long it will take or the price you'll have to pay, but you know in your heart that it will happen. By the time you reach this stage, you will have become a battle-tested, mentally tough warrior, and you'll have the emotional scars to prove it. You'll never forget the price you had to pay to become wealthy. Financial success is fantastic, but it's not free. Oh, and when your friends talk about your success when you're not around, they'll say you just got lucky. Welcome to the world of the self-made rich.

QUOTE:

"The price of being a sheep is boredom. The price of being a wolf is loneliness. Choose one or the other with great care." –Hugh Macleod

ACTION STEP:

Start reading one quote on success every day, and keep a collection of your favorites for future review.

CRITICAL THINKING QUESTION:

Are you willing to pay the price for extraordinary success while everyone else is playing around?

MILLIONAIRE RESOURCE:

Read Think and Grow Rich, by Napoleon Hill.

CHAPTER 4

Failure Isn't Fatal

Failure is the most misunderstood concept in business. Human beings are emotional animals that have an addiction to feeling important. Napoleon said; "Men will die for ribbons." We love to hold up our trophies, brag about our successes and bask in the glory of adoration. And while there's not anything inherently wrong with this, it's a serious weakness that cannot be overlooked. All that's necessary to defeat an emotional creature is to rob him of his ribbons and successes, and his fragile self-esteem begins to break down. This is why the masses play it safe and refuse to go for their dreams. They know deep down that if they fail, they will be emotionally devastated, because their self-worth is rooted in their successes, no matter how small or insignificant. It's a percentage play that protects their feelings of importance, and they guard it with their lives. Don't buy into it. According to studies, the number one deathbed regret is "I should have taken more chances and gone for my dreams." This is the sad ending for so many, and you don't want to be one of these people. Failure is not to be feared but merely treated as a part of the path to success. It isn't an indictment of who you are, your intelligence or your worth as a human being. It's simply an objective result to a given action; nothing more and nothing less. The failures you experience on your path to financial independence become the intellectual capital in which you will build your empire. Failure gives you feedback, and feedback makes you smarter. Failure is a friend that tells you the truth. If you avoid her, you're only hindering your growth. If you embrace her, she will teach you what doesn't work so you can figure out what does. Failure isn't fatal; it's vital to your success. Don't fear it. Expect it and learn its lessons.

QUOTE:

"Failure is simply the opportunity to begin again, this time more intelligently." –Henry Ford

ACTION STEP:

Interview three of the most successful adults your parents can introduce you to and ask them about the role failure has played in their success.

CRITICAL THINKING QUESTION:

What was your biggest failure and what did you learn from it?

MILLIONAIRE RESOURCE:

Read How I Raised Myself from Failure to Success in Selling, by Frank Bettger.

CHAPTER 5

Get Rich Solving Problems

You're going to hear all kinds of theories about how to become wealthy, mostly from people who have never done it. Politicians, pundits, and the press will say how difficult it is, especially in an interconnected, slow-growing, global economy. Don't believe it. The truth is that it's never been easier to get rich. This is due to the number of the new problems that have surfaced as technology has disrupted the world. The masses solve small problems for their employers. The rich solve significant problems and get compensated accordingly. Getting rich is not complicated. To the contrary, it's simple. Solve a big problem, and the world will gladly turn their money over to you. The world wants you to be rich because it has a lot of challenges to solve. The masses make the mistake of confusing something that's simple for something that's easy. To clarify, getting rich is NOT easy. If it were easy, everyone would be rich. It's not. But it is simple. If you want to be rich, solve a problem. If you want to be *very* wealthy, solve a bigger problem. The larger problem you solve, the richer you get. In a free market economy, that's all there is to it. Teachers, professors and the majority of the population don't believe this, so be ready for their denial. Many of these people are bright, highly educated and well intended. They're just ignorant on how wealth is created. While they are studying the way the world works, the wealthy are out there improving it. Don't waste your time trying to convince them that they're wrong. Remember, the underlying reason they cling to their negative beliefs about the rich and getting wealthy is the fear of failure. It's easier to criticize winners than it is to become one. As they're berating your ambition, keep in mind that someday they may be enjoying the fruits of your creation. Match your unique talents, abilities, and passions with a problem-solving idea, and you'll be on your way to wealth.

QUOTE:

"The bigger problem you solve, the more money you make" –Steve Siebold

ACTION STEP:

Make a list of the 3 biggest problems that you see in your school and 3 possible ideas to solve them.

CRITICAL THINKING QUESTION:

In school, are you a problem creator or a problem solver?

MILLIONAIRE RESOURCE:

Read Problem Solving 101, by Ken Watanabe

CHAPTER 6

Be a Producer

You'll probably hear from adults of influence that your generation is spoiled, entitled and lazy, and how their generation was bolder, tougher and more ambitious. Don't believe it. Every generation hears this from the previous generation. You'll hear tall tales of them walking to school in the freezing rain, sleet and snow. You'll hear how they always obeyed their parents and did as they were told. The fact is that every generation has spoiled, entitled and lazy people, and every generation has producers; the people who build, create, think and get things done. These are the winners in the world. They lead their generation, solve problems and sometimes even get rich. The producers have given us the greatest, most prosperous standard of living in the history of the world. To be a producer means bucking conventional thinking and societal dogma in exchange for progressive ideas. The downside is that the producers are always demonized before they are celebrated. Some are demonized their entire lives, and only vindicated posthumously. But no matter how long it takes for producers to be recognized, their impact is felt almost immediately. Producers determine their goal, decide what they want and then go get it. They are thought leaders looking for a better way, and when they find it, the journey to make it even better begins. They are usually years ahead of their time yet require no endorsement from anyone else to keep them engaged and on track. Decide in what capacity you will become a producer and then set out to make it happen. Do it because you love the process and not for the money or recognition, and that will ensure that you will persist until you succeed. Expect critics to attack you and be worried if they don't. Produce solutions to problems and expect the world to push back. Once you prove yourself, they will become your greatest champions.

QUOTE:

'The producers are the people who get things done. They drive invention, innovation, and progress. They are the heroes of any free market society." –Steve Siebold

ACTION STEP:

Research 3 of your favorite producers and list one thing that makes them unique.

CRITICAL THINKING QUESTION:

In your opinion, who is the greatest producer in history?

MILLIONAIRE RESOURCE:

Read Why the Rich are Getting Richer, by Robert Kiyosaki

CHAPTER 7

Money Won't Make You Happy

Financial independence is a wonderful thing. Being rich is even better. Building long-term wealth is life changing. But don't expect any of these things to make you happy. The masses spend most of their lives worrying about money and imagining how life would be on easy street. They'll tell you that money won't make you happy, yet they secretly believe it will. They're wrong, and mostly because they've never experienced it. Having money makes your life easier and more comfortable. It offers you opportunities you can't get in any other way. But if you're not happy without it, you won't be happy with it. Paying off your school loans and credit cards is a great feeling, but the feeling is fleeting. Building your dream house is amazing, but after the excitement wears off, it's still like any other house with bedrooms, bathrooms and a kitchen, only nicer. The most exhilarating moment of purchasing your fantasy car is the day before you pick it up. The fact is that emotional animals thrive on emotion, and while money can buy things that excite us, they rarely keep us happy. The happiest people are closely connected to others, such as friends and family, whom they travel through life together. The best strategy is to create your happiness before you create your wealth, and don't expect your financial success to have any sustainable long-term impact on your level of fulfillment and happiness. Making your life easier and more comfortable are good enough reasons to chase wealth. It will allow you to live life on your terms and timeline. The rich live by their own rules, and money gives you the freedom to make them up as you go. Without wealth, you'll always answer to someone who has it. With it, you'll answer only to yourself. Choose the road that gives you the comfort to live and the freedom to chart your own course.

QUOTE:

"Money can buy you a fine dog, but only love will make him wag his tail"—Kinky Friedman

ACTION STEP:

Make a list of the three things in life that create the most happiness for you.

CRITICAL THINKING QUESTION:

Are you counting on money and material things to make you happy?

MILLIONAIRE RESOURCE:

Subscribe to The Wall Street Journal, and ask your parents to read it with you.

CHAPTER 8

Rich People Are No Better

Some of the best people you'll ever meet won't be rich. They may be smart, educated and worldly, but not rich. It doesn't make them any less than someone who is rich. It usually just means they didn't spend much time focusing on money. You'll hear a lot from adults about how the rich think they're better than others, but it's not true at all. Some of this misunderstanding is generated by the fact that rich people tend to associate with other rich people. They often live in the same neighborhoods, join the same country clubs and attend the same charity events. This is because their status gives them access, not because they think they are better than anyone else. Wealthy people are the biggest philanthropists in the world, and their giving is voluntary. There's a lot of jealousy of the rich, which is another reason the masses like to demonize them. It's easier to criticize them than it is to become one of them. Anyone who's attempted to build their own fortune knows how tough it is, and even if they don't succeed, they respect the people who do. The wealthy also associate with other financial winners because they know that consciousness is contagious. Socializing with other wealthy people exposes them to big ideas, grand visions and fearless thinking. Many business deals are conducted at charity events, art auctions, golf outings, polo matches, tennis mixers and the like. The bottom line is that most self-made millionaires created their fortunes from scratch, the hard way. They ran the company, swept the floor and took out the garbage for years before breaking through. After they're successful, they can cut a deal on the golf course that makes them more money in a day than they did during their first 5 years in business. If you were in their place, wouldn't you associate with other rich people?

QUOTE:

"The way in which the rich are better than the poor and middle class is in their beliefs, habits and focus on money."

ACTION STEP:

List 5 events, clubs or groups that only rich people can get into.

CRITICAL THINKING QUESTION:

Do you understand the value of having access to rich and powerful people in a non-business environment?

MILLIONAIRE RESOURCE:

Read, (with your parents) How to Get Rich, by Felix Dennis

CHAPTER 9

Middle Class Equals Mediocrity

During the post-World War Two years, the middle class was a level of social status that American's strived to achieve. People dreamed of owning their own home and charting their own course. Today, being a member of the middle class is assumed by anyone with even a limited education and minimal focus on success. Inexpensive access to information, technology, and credit has raised the bar and opened the door to world-class success for anyone with the guts to go after it. You no longer need a Harvard degree or a Hollywood movie role to get rich. All you need is the drive; work ethic and solution to a problem people are willing to pay for. We are living in the golden age people have been dreaming about for hundreds of years, and that's why so many of us are out there staking our claim. All of this opportunity has lowered middle-class results to mediocrity. Many people in our society don't care about being rich. As long as they have a roof over their head and food to feed their family, they are satisfied. There's nothing wrong with not wanting to be rich, although it usually relegates people to a lifetime of struggle and worry. The truth is that unless you are born into poverty, your ascension to the middle class is almost guaranteed. You'll hear how important the middle class is to the economy and it's true. The masses need money to buy products and services to live even a minimal existence. That being said, aspiring to the middle class is outdated by decades. The ambitious people of today aspire to join the world-class, where they can write their own ticket and attain their wildest dreams. World-class wealth may not make you better or happier, but it will open the door to a life most people only see in movies. It's where you want to be, no matter what field you choose to take you there.

QUOTE:

"All good is hard. All evil is easy. Dying, losing, cheating and mediocrity is easy. Stay away from easy." –Scott Alexander

ACTION STEP:

Decide today to reject the idea that middle-class success is enough.

CRITICAL THINKING QUESTION:

Are you aiming for middle-class or world-class results?

MILLIONAIRE RESOURCE:

Read How To Be Rich, by J. Paul Getty

CHAPTER 10

Avoid Blood Money

There's a distinction between the classes that are important for you to understand. The masses tend to see rich people as belonging to the upper class, but there's a higher level. The upper class consists of affluent individuals who have a bank full of blood money. Blood money is acquired at the expense of others. Slave owners, sweatshop operators, and ruthless people in business are examples. The most common modern-day examples are people who abuse their power to gain wealth. They lie, cheat and steal their way to success, leaving their victims in the street to suffer. This is not the way you want to build your fortune. The poetic justice of blood money is that it often haunts the people who hurt others to attain it. They often end up alone and depressed. The only friends they have been bought, and many would turn their backs on them. The people that fail to experience remorse for acquiring blood money are sharks and sociopaths. The good news is that there's a higher level, which is world-class. These are people that build their fortunes through honesty, integrity, and service. Rather than leaving a trail full of victims, they enhance people's lives. These people are winners, and they're approach not only makes them rich, but it also helps them lead lives of fulfillment and happiness. Where the upper class operates from an ego-based consciousness, the world-class operates from a spirit-based consciousness. They treat people like they want to be treated and refuse to sacrifice others in the pursuit of their dreams. By observing the famous rich people in the media, you'll see how easy it is to identify the upper class from the world-class. Leave the blood where it belongs, and build your empire without harming anyone in the process.

QUOTE:

"If you have to hurt people to get rich, you're never going to enjoy your success."

ACTION STEP:

Write down three ways you can help people solve their problems in exchange for money.

CRITICAL THINKING QUESTION:

How would you feel about yourself if you became rich by hurting other people?

MILLIONAIRE RESOURCE:

Read Seven Choices for Success to Significance, by Dr. Nido Qubein.

CHAPTER 11

People Aren't Equal

You're going to hear teachers, politicians, sports coaches and others tell you that all people are equal. This is wishful thinking. Human beings are predisposed to make sense of a world that often doesn't make sense. This reduces the fear they feel from uncertainty. Sometimes they make ignorant, thoughtless statements that lack truth or evidence in an attempt to ease their emotional insecurities. I'm not speaking of equality among the races, because in reality, there is only one race, and that is the human race. We should all be treated with equal respect and equal justice, but that does not make us equal in any other way. Some people are born smarter, while others possess superior athletic or artistic talent. Certain people excel in academics, and others are gifted with mechanical abilities. Every human being is a unique blend of talent and ability. The same goes for the genders. We've been brainwashed to believe men and women are equal, which is more wishful thinking from the masses. The fact is that women are superior in some ways to men, and vice versa. Men and women are both parts of the human race and should be treated equally, but they are not many other ways. Equality is just one of the many myths of the masses, and you want to avoid buying into it. Every human being has a set of unique talents, and your job is to find your own and leverage them to construct the life you desire. Never expect equal pay unless you provide equal service. Create superior service, and you will reap superior rewards. This is how you join the wealthy in the winner's circle. Not through some myth of the masses, but by being unequal in the value that you provide.

QUOTE:

"The worst form of in inequality is to try to make unequal thing equal"
—Aristotle

ACTION STEP:

Decide today to treat everyone as equals as you strive to become unequal.

CRITICAL THINKING QUESTION:

Does being better at something make you a better human being?

MILLIONAIRE RESOURCE:

Read: One Another's Equals: The Basis of Human Equality, by Jeremy Waldron

CHAPTER 12

The World is Beautiful and Brutal

You're going to hear a lot of things about the world we live in from people with good intentions. Some of the things you hear will be true, and others will once again fall into the category of wishful thinking. To be successful, you need to be grounded in the truth, so you don't belong to the delusion of the masses. The fact is that the world is a complicated place with a long history of war, brutality, beauty, and love. Human beings have made brilliant advances in every aspect of life, yet we still haven't figured out how to stop killing each other. History reveals the world that is both horrific and hopeful, and most likely, that will never change. The key is to know the facts of the world you're entering into so you can successfully navigate it. The fact that you or your parents have enough discretionary income to purchase this book places you among the world's most prosperous people. The bottom line is you've been lucky enough to be born into the right place at the right time. This gives you an enormous advantage over the majority of the people on the planet. Be grateful for your good fortune, but don't feel guilty. Just resolve to make the most of your luck and don't waste it watching television and playing video games. Treat entertainment as the dessert portion of the meal, while treating your work as the main course. And if you decide to be a stay at home mom, raising kids will be your job. The point is to capitalize on the lottery-ticket-like life in which you've been given. 99% of the world would do anything to have the unlimited opportunity you were born into. Don't fritter it away like most people. Go out into the world and stake your claim, make your mark, and if you're so inclined, lend a hand or two to people who are not as fortunate as you are. Take responsibility for your own life. It's all up to you.

QUOTE:

"Here is the world. Beautiful and terrible things will happen. Don't be afraid."—Frederick Buechner

ACTION STEP:

Decide to see the world as it is, not what you wish it were.

CRITICAL THINKING QUESTION:

As it relates to the truth of how the world works, is there a cost to delusional thinking?

MILLIONAIRE RESOURCE:

Read: Sapiens: A Brief History of Humankind, by Yuval Noah Harari

CHAPTER 13

Government is Not Your Friend

Government's role in the United States is supposed to be limited in scope and focused on protecting citizens from foreign and domestic threats. It also brings people together to collectively create infrastructure none of us could afford on our own. The problem is that government continues to grow, create more laws, and forces us to pay more in taxes so it can overspend in almost every area. The government is not inherently evil, but its blood thirst for control and power is. The government does some good things. Some of the laws and regulations protect the poor, disabled and struggling. It's an overstatement to say its all bad. But make no mistake, as a high-achiever, the government will want as much of your money as it can legally pilfer. This is why you must take government seriously and learn all that you can about how it works so you can stay out of its crosshairs. Make sure you understand the current tax code and how it impacts your income. Build a solid relationship with your accountant, because he/she's going to be the one who professionally navigates the system for you. Your accountant will teach you how to legally employ all of the strategies possible to minimize what the government takes. The good news is that America has a history of favoring the producers who create products and services, as well as those who employ people. Even Washington realizes that the country needs to take care of the people who produce, as opposed to the people who simply feed off of the system. As a wealthy person, you can expect to have a love-hate relationship with the U.S. Government. That being said, it's so large and powerful that your best strategy is to study it, so you understand what you're up against. The masses can barely get themselves to vote for President every four years; many don't even know the difference between the Constitution and the Declaration of Independence. Don't make this mistake. Study, watch, and even get involved in government if you are so inclined. But never ignore an entity with this much power.

QUOTE:

"Government's view of the economy could be summed up in a few short phrases: If it moves, tax it. If it keeps moving, regulate it. And if it stops moving, subsidize it." –President Ronald Reagan

ACTION STEP:

Ask your parents to help you read through a book called Independent Contractor, Sole Proprietor and LLC Taxes Explained, by Mike Piper

CRITICAL THINKING QUESTION:

How much might it cost you if you were to trust the government to always act in your best interests, financially?

MILLIONAIRE RESOURCE:

Read: The United States Constitution And The Fascinating Facts About It, by Terry Jordan

CHAPTER 14

Watch Wall Street and Main Street

As a self-made millionaire, you're going to learn an odd truth, which is that it's easier to *earn* money than it is to keep it. When you're rich, everyone wants a piece of your fortune, including the Bulls and Bears on Wall Street. Investing in the stock market is not for amateurs. As a matter of fact, even the professionals have a tough time making consistent profits. The smartest money earned on Wall Street is made by the money managers getting paid to oversee huge sums. They get paid a percentage of the money they manage whether or not their investments are successful. It's a good place to be. So if that becomes your profession, you'll already know the game. If not, treat Wall Street like the casino it is and precede with caution. Trying to time the market by predicting when stocks will rise, and fall is like walking into a casino in Las Vegas and randomly placing bets on slot machines. It's risky. The greatest investment advice you'll ever get is "Don't lose money," which is another way of saying only bet on sure things, so the worst you can do is maintain the principle with which you started. Keep up with what's happening every day on Wall Street. Study money and markets as much as you can so you know what's going on and can identify opportunities when they present themselves. Read the Wall Street Journal every day. In addition to Wall Street, also keep your eyes on Main Street. Know what's happening in your neighborhood. Ask the local shopkeepers how they're doing, what challenges they're facing and opportunities they're searching for. Use this intimate knowledge of local businesses to spot hot money making opportunities and long-term investments. Remember that big business is not the only place to invest your money. Sometimes opportunity is right around the corner from where you live. So always keep your eyes on what's happening around you. Talk to people, ask questions and you'll be surprised and pleased at how much you learn.

QUOTE:

"Rule No. 1: Never Lose Money. Rule No. 2: Never Forget Rule No. 1."—Warren Buffet

ACTION STEP:

Research and purchase stock in a company.

CRITICAL THINKING QUESTION:

Do you the discipline to invest your money unemotionally?

MILLIONAIRE RESOURCE:

Read: A Beginners Guide to Investing, by Alex Frey

CHAPTER 15

Think Hard

The hardest work in the world is thinking. It's also the highest *paid* work. I'm not talking about the thinking that the masses have made famous. Memorizing batting averages, box scores and Super Bowl stats won't do you much good. Thinking of solutions to problems people will pay for, will. Working hard is overrated. If hard work were the answer to getting rich, every cocktail waitress and construction worker would be a millionaire. The masses labor; while the rich, leverage. Thinking is a form of leverage, and it's the hardest work you'll ever do. It pays well because so few people are willing to do it, and the ones that do aren't very good. Build the habit of thinking big around solutions in the field you choose. Anyone can think small, but it takes courage, confidence, and even a hint of craziness to dream of solutions that scare most people. The more expertise you develop in your field, the bigger solutions you will discover. This is one of the reasons you want to be a specialist in an area that blends your talents and passions. This will ensure that you enjoy the process of creation and not just the paycheck.

Train yourself to keep thinking nonstop as long as you can, and eventually, you will develop the habit of perpetual thought. This gives you a significant advantage over your peers, most of which are thinking more about pleasure and entertainment than money and success. If this sounds like all work and no fun, it's not. You'll know when you need a break. And when you do, take it. But once you're rested, get back to thinking solutions and strategies. That's every rich person's primary role. Once your thinking generates a solution, you turn it over to your team for implementation. You don't really believe Bill Gates writes computer code, do you? Or that Warren Buffet calls in his own stock trades? Or that Steve Jobs actually built the iPod or iPhone with his own hands? Of course, they didn't. What they did was use the power of their minds to create the solutions, and that's how they got rich. Your job is to do the same.

QUOTE:

"Wealth is the product of man's capacity to think." –Ayn Rand

ACTION STEP:

Visit a Flotation Tank Center and float for an hour in a sensory deprived environment. This will illuminate the power of your mind when distractions are removed.

CRITICAL THINKING QUESTION:

What are you wasting your creative thought power thinking about?

MILLIONAIRE RESOURCE:

Read: Mindset: The New Psychology of Success, by Carol S. Dweck, Ph.D.

CHAPTER 16

Expect To Be Rich

Almost every self-made I've interviewed over the past 30+ years has told me he expected to be rich. You'll want to do the same. Start telling yourself now that based on the country in which you were born, the family you were born into, and the specific knowledge you have acquired, that you expect to be wealthy. Expect to get rich in your 20's or 30's. There's no need to wait until you have gray hair to stake your claim. It's not going to happen overnight, but it doesn't have to take a lifetime. Your expectation will quicken the process and keep you on track. Don't be afraid to tell people about your big plans, but be prepared to suffer the social fall-out if you do. Most people are taught to believe that wanting to be rich makes you shallow, self-absorbed and selfish. Don't be surprised when they react negatively for expressing a desire that most have yet lacked the courage to admit. Even in America, it's politically incorrect to express your financial ambitions if they're big goals. It's socially acceptable if you say you want to make a comfortable living, but when you say you want to be rich, it makes many people squirm. Try to identify people who support your ambitions and will encourage you to pursue them. You can build your expectation without the support of others, but it will grow faster if you surround yourself with people with similar vision. Read books, attend seminars, research online, and use any other method at your disposal to associate with other kids like you who are being groomed to be rich. Together, you will strengthen each other's expectations and distance yourself from the mediocre thinking of the masses. You will also begin to build relationships with kids who are going to become rich and powerful adults. Someday, when you need help solving a problem, you will be able to phone them and get help. Knowing a lot of people is good, but knowing a lot of rich and powerful people, is even better and more strategic.

QUOTE:

"In order to win, you must expect to win." –Richard Bach

ACTION STEP:

Starting today, begin telling yourself every day that you expect to be rich.

CRITICAL THINKING QUESTION:

With all the training and resources you have at your disposal, what would stop you from becoming a self-made millionaire?

MILLIONAIRE RESOURCE:

Read: Expect to Win, by Monte Holm (2nd Edition)

CHAPTER 17

Family First

One of the most important decisions you'll have to make is how to balance your time between work and family. For most people this is easy, but you are *not* most people. You're a self-made millionaire in the making, and that requires a greater investment of time, effort and dedication. While most people are spending their weekends working on their yard, at the beach or watching the game, you'll be working, thinking and planning. That's the price you'll pay for remarkable success. The problem is that being rich isn't going to make you happy. No matter how rich you become, you're going to want to share your life with people you love. Success is wonderful, but it's not enough to truly live the good life. For that, you're going to need family and friends, and to do that you'll need to find a way to create, cultivate and maintain healthy and happy relationships. This takes time and effort, but if you don't invest it, you're going to end up living alone in your water-front mansion wondering why you're so rich and miserable. First and foremost, find someone you care about who supports your ambition and encourages your dreams. Search for someone who understands you and celebrates your differences from the average person. Ultimately, your perfect mate will be someone who sees you as a hero that dares to stake his claim. She may not say it to you in the beginning, but you will see it in her eyes. It's a level of respect most people would die for and very few receive. Ideally, your mate will expect you to be as successful as you do. The reality is, that like it or not, the person you fall in love with is going to have an enormous influence on you and the way you think. Loving someone makes you emotionally vulnerable, and that's why it's critical to whom you expose yourself. Most people look for a mate with a pretty face and pleasing personality, but not you. You need more. You need a true partner that understands your mission and will be there for you during the tough times. You need a serious person that loves you more than life itself, and you cannot afford to accept anything less. Once you find this person, her needs must be placed above your ambitions. Sometimes this will be tough, but it will be worth it. Make this a personal motto: Family first, ambition second. If you get this one wrong, you'll end up rich and lonely.

QUOTE:

"Your family is your reason to win, not your excuse to fail"—Monte Holm

ACTION STEP:

Make a list of 10 traits you would like in a significant other.

CRITICAL THINKING QUESTION:

As it relates to your success, what are the three most important traits you would value in a significant other?

MILLIONAIRE RESOURCE:

Google: "Choosing a supportive significant other" and read a few of the articles.

CHAPTER 18

Treat People Well

As a self-made millionaire, you're going to be in a powerful position. You're going to make decisions that impact people's lives. Little things that wouldn't affect your life as a wealthy person will make a huge difference to them. As a result, it will be easy to make these decisions, but I advise you to make them cautiously and carefully and to consider how they will help or hurt others. The golden rule is best: treat others the way you wish to be treated. That says it all, but it's easy to say and harder to do. Remember that with great wealth comes great responsibility. Great wealth doesn't change people; it merely reveals their character. When you have power, only the strength of your character will keep you from abusing it. It's easy to scream at your employees when you're holding their paycheck in your hand, but that doesn't make it right. What if the situation were reversed? What would you think of a rich boss who sloppily and unapologetically wielded his power without regard for the feelings of others? It's not nice or necessary. Never allow your ego to convince you that the guy eating the food in the four-star restaurant is any better than the guy serving it. Just because you're rich doesn't mean you're better (or worse) than anyone else. I'm not suggesting that you apologize for your success. On the contrary, you should be proud of it. All I'm saying is that you're going to be able to get away with treating people poorly due to your position and status, and I'm imploring you not to take advantage of it. Treat the server the same as the person running the restaurant, and treat the maids who clean your mansion the same as the rich and powerful guests who frequent it. Not only is this the right thing to do, but it will also make you a happier and more fulfilled human being.

QUOTE:

"You're never too important to be nice to people"—Jon Batiste

ACTION STEP:

Begin treating people as you wish to be treated.

CRITICAL THINKING QUESTION:

How does the way you treat people affect the way you feel about yourself?

MILLIONAIRE RESOURCE:

Read: Treating People Well: The Extraordinary Power of Civility at Work and in Life, by Lea Berman and Jeremy Bernard

CHAPTER 19

Your Net Worth is Not Your Self Worth

When you're rich, people are going treat you differently. They're going to interact with as if you're royalty because, in the eyes of the average American, the rich and famous are the closest thing we have to royalty. People are going to go to great lengths to say yes to anything you ask of them, and only on rare occasions will anyone below your socioeconomic status say no. This is what life is like for the wealthy, and while it sounds like a dream, it can also be a trap. First and foremost, don't buy into it. You're *not* royalty, and you're no more special than the guy working on the back of a garbage truck. Never allow the masses to suck you into an egotistical, narcissistic mindset by making you feel that you're better than others. This happens all the time to the Nuevo Riche', the people with new money that start believing everyone who tells them how great they are. Some people will praise you because they genuinely respect your accomplishments, and others will have an ulterior motive. Be on the look out for both, because if you begin to believe them, you are headed down a dark path of psychological destruction. The end result is that you start to judge your own self-worth based on your net worth, and when you experience financial setbacks, your self-confidence, and sense of worthiness as a human being can crash along with your portfolio. Many millionaires have made this mistake, and some have never recovered. When your money is tied directly to your self-esteem, they go up and down together. When they're going up, it's never enough, and when they're going down, they may never return. Rich, poor or middle class, your worth as a human being is equal to anyone on the planet, and you need to believe that to be psychologically sound. No amount of success or failure can change your worthiness. Your worth is objective and indisputable. Once you understand and embrace these facts, you have a platform on which to build your self-confidence. When you take the calculated risks associated with financial success, sometimes you win, and other times you lose. The secret is to respond to both winning and losing in the same way. When you win; be grateful and recognize that you could have lost. When you lose; be grateful that it wasn't as bad as it could have been and move on with class and confidence. These are strategies the rich use to bounce back, move forward, and maintain they're psychological well-being.

QUOTE:

"When your self-worth goes up, your net worth goes up with it"—Mark Victor Hansen

ACTION STEP:

List three things that make you successful and three things that make you a good person, and they must be different from one another.

CRITICAL THINKING QUESTION:

On a scale of 1-7, 7 being best, how effective are you at separating what you do from whom you are?

MILLIONAIRE RESOURCE:

Read: Worthy: Boost Your Self Worth to Grow Your Net Worth, by Nancy Levin

CHAPTER 20

Dream about Money

Most people think about negatively about money. The majority of people see money as a necessary evil they are forced to handle. Their experience with money is limited to scrounging and saving every penny to make ends meet. They endure sleepless nights suffering and worrying about how they're going to afford to pay for school, rent, and food. And this ongoing nightmare usually lasts a lifetime. This is not for you. You're being groomed for greatness, and that means doing the opposite of the masses. Millionaires don't have nightmares about money; they have *dreams* about money. They dream of what life will be like at the next level, no matter how rich they are. They are always dreaming about the next conquest, idea, product or program that will catapult them to previously unimagined heights. They dream of how it will feel to reach the next peak along the summit, and then they transfer that excitement into their work. They're excited because they always have something to which to look forward. As soon as they manifest their current dream, they create another one. The self-made rich never rest on their laurels, because they've figured out the secret that the masses don't understand: that success is not about money, recognition or material rewards: it's about how it makes you feel. It's about how it makes you feel to set a goal and accomplish it. It's about the person you become along the path to success rather than the success itself. As you achieve goal after goal, even amidst failures along the way, you begin to believe you can do anything, and no house you'll ever own or car you'll ever drive will feel better than that. Success makes you feel ten feet and bullet proof, and that's a feeling most people never experience. This will be your life as a producer, a winner, and a champion.

QUOTE:

"Money is not the goal. Money has no value. The value comes from the dreams money helps achieve."—Robert Kiyosaki

ACTION STEP:

Write down the three biggest dreams you have that only money can buy.

CRITICAL THINKING QUESTION:

Are you dreaming randomly or are you dreaming of the future?

MILLIONAIRE RESOURCE:

Read: Dreams: Interpreting Your Dreams and How to Dream Your Desires, by Victoria Price

CHAPTER 21

Decide How Much is Enough

There are two types of rich people: those that decide how much money is enough and those that always need more. I've spent a lot of time with both groups, and the people that decide how much is enough tend to feel more fulfilled. Now when I suggest that you decide how much is enough, I don't mean that you have to stop building your portfolio or close down your shop. To the contrary, the day you hit the number you determine to be enough, is the day you *really* get dangerous! If you thought you were focused before, wait until every profit you make goes off to your favorite church, charity or cause. You may decide to bolster your personal fortune, which is fine. The point is that once you reach the number you have predetermined to be enough, you begin to see making money as a game instead of survival or a success mechanism. Now you're just playing for fun, and once making money becomes a game, you no longer fear the ups and downs of acquiring, investing and growing it. The people that claim to need more often don't actually *need* more, they just *want* more, and the reason is often to feed an inferiority complex. The world is full of examples. The greatest case study of a public figure I've made along these lines is Donald Trump. No matter how much success he achieves or how much money he makes, it's never enough. He always wants more, and this is what leads him to make statements such as what we heard during the 2016 Presidential election and even into his Presidency. Donald Trump is a smart, well-educated, successful man. The childish behavior he exhibits and braggadocios statements he makes stem from a deep-rooted inferiority complex he's never transcended. Until he does, he will always need more. He will spend the rest of his life pouring more success and money into a hole that cannot be filled. It's sad but true, and this is why I want you to avoid it. Decide how much is enough, go get it, and then play the game for fun.

QUOTE:

"Experience has taught us that material wants know no natural bounds, that they will expand without end unless we consciously restrain them. Capitalism rests precisely on this endless expansion of wants. That is why, for all its success, it remains so unloved. It has given us wealth beyond measure, but has taken away the chief benefit of wealth: the consciousness of having enough." —Robert Skidelsky

ACTION STEP:

Make an annual list of all the things you want to buy, do and experience and what they cost. This will give you an idea of how much you need.

CRITICAL THINKING QUESTION:

Does it serve your best interests to wish for more or wish for enough?

MILLIONAIRE RESOURCE:

Read: How Much is Enough? Money and the Good Life, by Robert Skidelsky and Edward Skidelsky

CHAPTER 22

Decide Who You Want To Be

You're going to be rich. It's only a matter of time. Start thinking about how you're going to represent yourself in the world and whom you want to be. To be rich after a lifetime of effort is one thing, but being young and rich is another. You're going to be a role model for your generation, and even older people are going to look up to you. How will you act? How will you speak? Will you play the cocky and cool know it all or the grateful and humble champion? These are decisions you need to make long before you stake your claim and make your fortune. It's your life, and it will be your decision, but consider the idea that the world doesn't need another brash young billionaire that acts as if she is smarter and better than everyone else. The world needs role models of self-made young men and women that have as much character as they do money. The world needs successful people who make others feel like they can do the same. You're going to have a backstage pass to every party, event and gala money can buy, and the richer you become, the more camera's will be flashing in your face. When these photos show up in the press, what will some impressionable young person glean from them? What will it say about you? Although they hate to admit it, American's have always worshipped at the altar of success. In a lifetime of traveling the world, I've never experienced a culture so enamored with winning and winners. Maybe that's one of the reasons our nation is so successful. But when you *become* one of the winners and people are putting you on a pedestal, will they be led down the right path or dead end street? Will you disappoint them or remain a hero? The world needs fewer ballers and more heroes. You can be a shining star yet remain modest, hard working and down to earth. This is part of you're grooming to become a self-made millionaire, but it will be your choice whether or not to implement the lessons you've learned.

QUOTE:

"Nearly all men can stand adversity, but if you want to test a man's character, give him power." –Abraham Lincoln

ACTION STEP:

List the 5 character traits you admire most.

CRITICAL THINKING QUESTION:

Who inspires you: the boastful braggart or the humble giant?

MILLIONAIRE RESOURCE:

Read: What Do You Stand For? For Teens: A Guide to Building Character, by Barbara Lewis

CHAPTER 23

Think for Yourself

The best form of education society has discovered over the years is to expose children to a series of institutions (schools) and people of influence (teachers) to help mold them into successful, self-reliant adults. And for the most part, it works. The truth is the system successfully teaches children how to memorize facts and figures, and think as the people and institutions that taught them. The net result of our system, when it works, is a well-adjusted, well-spoken, average thinking adult. And for most people, that's fine. But not for you. You're being prepared for greatness, and following the system that creates clones is not going to work. Most people you'll encounter in the years of your upbringing will be well educated, well intended, yet struggling adults giving you the best they have to offer. Teachers, coaches, clergy, Boy and Girl Scout leaders, parents of your friends and others will teach you what they know. The problem is you can't give someone something you don't have. The odds are that most of these people won't know the first thing about getting rich, and many will look down on the wealthy. You're training in this area will place you well above most of them, and that's going to make it necessary to ignore much of their advice around winning and wealth. The average person is taught *what* to think. The millionaire in the making is taught *how* to think, and that's what separates the classes. Don't be angry with your teachers for not being well versed in the language of success. Even college professors are doing a tough job for a pitiful salary, and most of them put their hearts and souls into it. As a self-made millionaire, you're going to make more money in a week than they make in a year. So be kind and respectful, and take away all the lessons they can teach you because many will be valuable. But...also think for yourself. Gather all the evidence you can and reach your own conclusions, which may be the polar opposite of your professors. Self-made millionaires usually don't follow the traditional trail; they blaze their own. That doesn't mean the masses are always wrong about life in general, but they are *usually* wrong about money. That's one of the reasons they struggle to survive in a country where the streets are paved with gold. Think for yourself and decide for yourself. Not as an act of rebellion, but as an act of prudence.

QUOTE:

"Take the risk of thinking for yourself, much more happiness, truth beauty, and wisdom will come to you that way." —Christopher Hitchens

ACTION STEP:

Write down three things you've been taught by adults of influence that you know are self-limiting, self-destructive, or wrong.

CRITICAL THINKING QUESTION:

If most adults are so smart, why aren't they rich?

MILLIONAIRE RESOURCE:

Read: Thinking for Yourself: Developing Critical Thinking Skills through Reading and Writing, by Marlys Mayfield

CHAPTER 24

Avoid Magical Thinking

"Things always work out for the best." "Justice always prevails." "You can do anything you set your mind to." These are all examples of magical thinking, a process in which emotional creatures love to indulge. Magical thinking comforts people during turbulent times. And for the more desperate, it keeps them from jumping off of buildings. Despite these benefits, magical thinking has little grounding in facts; it's simply made up to help people make sense of the random nature of life. This is fine for most people. All the average person is trying to do is survive and avoid pain. The ultimate goal of the masses is to be comfortable, and magical thinking is one way they achieve it. This is not for you. Deluding yourself in fairy tales is not how you achieve world-class success. The secret is living your life in objective reality, or as close as you can get to it. This is easier said than done. Life can brutal, and the world can be a nasty place, but these are the conditions in which you have to operate. Your job is to see the world as it is, not as you wish it were. If magical thinking were rooted in reality, it would be wonderful. But magic doesn't exist. The closest thing you're going to get to magic is the transformation of your own consciousness, and fortunately, that's something you can control. As you strike out on your own to get rich, enter your field of choice with clear eyes and see it for what it truly is. Dissect it from top to bottom to determine its potential. Of course, you want to pursue your passion, but if your passion is underwater basket weaving, you're going to have a tough time getting rich. The objective reality in the market place shows there is little demand for underwater weavers. The next step is to be objective about your talents and skills. If you're lousy at math, a career in engineering is probably not for you. Never delude yourself into believing you're better at something than you really are. That's what the masses do, and it's a big reason that most of them are broke. Grounding your thinking in objective reality, while avoiding self-delusion and magical thinking is a skill you develop over time. Start now, and by the time you're ready to take on the world, you'll be a master.

QUOTE:

"A dream doesn't become a reality through magic; it takes sweat, determination and hard work." –Colin Powell

ACTION STEP:

List three sayings you've heard that you would describe as magical thinking.

CRITICAL THINKING QUESTION:

Why does magical thinking make people happy while keeping them broke?

MILLIONAIRE RESOURCE:

Read: SUPERSENSE: Why We Believe In The Unbelievable, by Bruce M. Hood

CHAPTER 25

Make Rich Friends

The masses don't believe that the heart of every self-made millionaire's success is in the way they think. The masses think rich people have gamed the system, or that the system itself, is rigged. The fact is rich people think very differently than the average person, most notably, as it relates to money, investing, and acquiring wealth. That's why you need rich friends. The sheer exposure to their heightened level of awareness around everything related to wealth will dramatically expand your thinking. Rich people make friends and associate with other rich people, just like any other ethnic, social, or minority group. They understand each other because they live in the same world. Attend a cocktail party in an average neighborhood, and you'll spend the evening talking about football scores, video games or the latest movies. Attend a cocktail party in an affluent neighborhood, and you're bound to bump into politicians, business leaders and millionaires discussing deals, government regulation, and financial markets. More deals are done at informal gatherings than in boardrooms. There's a bond that's created between rich people because, like any other minority, they are often unfairly villainized and discriminated against. As a result, rich people stick together. The most common thing you'll hear at a social event with rich people is "I might be able to help you." And this comes from people who would normally be next to impossible to reach in any other way. The masses like to say that it's not what you know, but whom you know. The truth is that it's *who knows you*, and how many of these people are willing to help you. Wealthy people do not suffer fools gladly. If you're not a top performer, they will be nice to you, but you'll never do business together. Begin cultivating relationships with rich people as soon as possible. Read their books, attend their events, donate to their charities, move into their neighborhoods, join their clubs and whatever else you can do to gain introductions and build relationships.

QUOTE:

"The richest people in the world look for and build networks. Everyone else looks for work." –Robert Kiyosaki

ACTION STEP:

Interview a self-made millionaire in the next 90 days.

CRITICAL THINKING QUESTION:

People target friends that share their passion for sports, entertainment, and music. Is there anything wrong with befriending people share your passion for success?

MILLIONAIRE RESOURCE:

Read: Here's How Rich People Choose Their Friends, published by Business Insider. Available at http://www.businessinsider.com/rich-people-choose-friends-2014-12

CHAPTER 26

Money Solves Most Problems

Being rich won't make you happy, but it will solve 90% of your problems. If you have a problem, and you can make it disappear by writing a check, you *don't* have a problem. And most problems can be purchased and eliminated. You'll hear the masses say that money is no help if you have advanced heart disease or cancer. Not always true. In some cases, money can save your life. Many countries outside the United States offer life-saving medicine, treatments, and surgeries that our government refuses to approve. If someone is sick and finds a cure overseas, the average person can't do much about it. But all that a millionaire has to do is pack her bags and fly wherever she needs to go and stay as long as she needs to stay. Is it fair that the average person may die from the same disease the rich person flew to France to be cured of? No, it's not. Life isn't fair. It never has been and never will be. That's objective reality minus magical thinking. We all wish life were a level playing field, but it's not. Don't buy into the philosophy that it's noble to die from a disease you could have saved yourself from simply because people with less money couldn't afford it. There is no nobility in self-denial or self-destruction. Make your money by solving problems, and you'll get rich enough to purchase your own problems away. This is one of the biggest advantages of being rich, and since you will have earned every penny, you'll never need to apologize for utilizing it.

QUOTE:

"Never stress over problems that can be purchased."

ACTION STEP:

List three major problems in life that be solved with money.

CRITICAL THINKING QUESTION:

If money solves most problems, is it prudent to deny its importance?

MILLIONAIRE RESOURCE:

MONEY Master The Game: 7 Simple Steps to Financial Freedom, by Tony Robbins

CHAPTER 27

Invest

The average person makes little money and spends more than they earn. They rack up thousands of dollars in credit card debt and pay an average of 22% in annual interest. This is not for you. Rich people don't spend more than they make and rarely carry high interest loans. The rich are *investors*, not spenders. They invest their money today, so they'll have more tomorrow. The rich invest in what they refer to as "sure things," which usually means investing in areas they know well. Self-made millionaires rarely get rich through investing; they get rich solving problems. Investing allows them to grow their wealth as they create it. You're going to see people fritter away their wealth by building enormous homes, buying exotic cars, private planes, expensive jewelry and just about every other toy you can imagine. These people tend to be young, uneducated and from poor socioeconomic backgrounds. Professional football and basketball players, boxers, artists, actors and other newly minted millionaires that believe their money train is going to last forever. An alarming percentage of them end up filing for bankruptcy and never recover. Your job is to study investment areas in which you have interest. If you like to play guitars, you might study the vintage guitar market. If you're a baseball fan, look into investing in rare baseball cards. If you like dissecting stocks, you could study the stock market. There are endless areas to invest in, and the more you know about the market in which you're investing, the safer and more profitable your returns will be. Investing is not as easy as most people think, and that's why you want to start now and learn as much as you can.

QUOTE:

"The amount of money you have has got nothing to do with what you earn. People earning a million dollars a year can have no money. People earning $35,000 a year can be quite well off. It's not what you earn, it's what you spend." — Paul Clitheroe

ACTION STEP:

Write down three areas you would be passionate about investing in.

CRITICAL THINKING QUESTION:

What is your favorite hobby, interest or activity, and is there a way you can invest in it?

MILLIONAIRE RESOURCE:

Read: The Motley Fool Investment Guide for Teens: 8 Steps to Having More Money Than Your Parents Ever Dreamed Of, by David and Tom Gardner

CHAPTER 28

Stay Open Minded

Most people close their minds to new ideas as they get older. Many believe they've discovered the way the world works, and they distance themselves from new approaches. As a future self-made millionaire, you should do the opposite. Always keep your eyes, ears, and mind open to new ideas and opportunities. Society is evolving at a rapidly increasing rate, and it's only going to get faster. Technology has disrupted the way we do business and the way we live, and the next seismic shift is right around the corner. While the masses are paralyzed from the unprecedented pace of change, the rich are capitalizing on it by creating solutions to the new problems these changes are creating. This is the path you want to follow. The more disruption occurs, the more problems that need to be solved, and the richer you can become. Staying open-minded means you're always looking for ways to become more successful. Investments, business opportunities, partnerships, joint ventures, new products and services and anything else that may bolster your bank account. Even the smallest idea can become profitable to someone with an open mind who can visualize the product or service in action. The average person prejudges new opportunities based on their knowledge of the past, and this can be a costly habit. Keep an open mind your entire career, and you'll be pleasantly surprised at some of the unexpected outcomes you experience.

QUOTE:

"Open minded people embrace being wrong, are free of Illusions, don't mind what people think of them, and question everything, including themselves."

ACTION STEP:

Identify one major belief you have and challenge its validity by studying the opposing view.

CRITICAL THINKING QUESTION:

If you were more open minded, would you be more successful?

MILLIONAIRE RESOURCE:

https://www.authentichappiness.sas.upenn.edu/newsletters/authentichappinesscoaching/open-mindedness

CHAPTER 29

Understand Capitalism

Capitalism is a system where private owners, instead of the government, control the country's trade and industry. It's the system that built the most prosperous country in the history of the world. Over the years, the United States government has continuously interfered with and attempted to water down our capitalistic system through over regulation, excessive taxation and by creating laws that make it more difficult for small business owners to succeed. All of this is done in the name of power, based on the philosophy that the government knows what's best for the American public. It doesn't, but the power grab will continue to choke off new opportunities to become wealthy. This is one of the reasons you need to become a global citizen, so you understand where the economic opportunities exist, and how to profit from them. The average person has no idea or interest in building a global investment portfolio, and this is a mistake that will continue to become more costly as more of our hard earned money is stolen by the looters in Washington. Capitalism is being adopted by poor countries with emerging markets across the world, and it's succeeding. When business people are untangled from bureaucratic interference and are free to create and sell products and services to consumers who wish to purchase them, everyone wins. Capitalism is not perfect, and one of the reasons our government is so intrusive is because some of the big businesses in the past have taken advantage and profited from unknowing, vulnerable consumers. This has given our government an excuse to stick their noses into every business owners' windows attempting to monitor and regulate every move we make. As a future millionaire, you need to study capitalism, government over reach, emerging markets, and anything related to building, investing and sheltering your wealth. It's tedious and time-consuming, yet it's an important habit to start building immediately.

QUOTE:

"Capitalism needs neither propaganda nor apostles. Its achievements speak for themselves. Capitalism delivers the goods." –Ludwig von Mises

ACTION STEP:

Start a small business venture and set a goal to become profitable within your first 12 months in business.

CRITICAL THINKING QUESTION:

What are the three most positive elements of a capitalistic society?

MILLIONAIRE RESOURCE:

Read: Capitalism for Kids: Growing Up To Be Your Own Boss, by Karl Hess

CHAPTER 30

Use Other Peoples Money

Rich people are always looking for places to invest their money. Many of them believe it's easier to make money than it is to invest and grow it, and that opens up the opportunity to people that structure unique financial vehicles for the rich to invest their money. You can invest ten million dollars of your own money on a strip mall in Costa Rica, or you can invest one million dollars of your own money and nine million from other investors. Savvy investors use other people's money to mitigate risk. Sometimes you'll be able to structure deals where you don't have to invest any of your own capital, which is even better. Your goal as a wealthy investor is to reduce your exposure to potential losses while diversifying your portfolio. Think of it this way: let's say there's construction work going on in your neighborhood, and during the summer, those workers get thirsty from the heat. Being the future millionaire you are, you see the opportunity to cash in by opening a lemonade stand in your front yard. You determine it's going to cost about $40 dollars for a week's worth of lemonade plus cups and other supplies. You have $40 dollars in your savings account, but that's every penny you have. Instead of taking on 100% of the risk, you ask your dad to invest the $40 while you work the stand all day, and you split the profits. Your father supplies the capital, and you provide the labor as a 50-50 partnership. If it succeeds, you both profit. It if fails to return the original $40 dollars, your dad takes the loss, and you worked for free. Not a great outcome, but consider this: Your $40 is still safely tucked away. That's one example of using other people's money, and it's done by millionaire investor's every day.

QUOTE:

"Business, that's easily defined—its other people's money." –Peter Drucker

ACTION STEP:

Ask your parents to structure a business deal with you as your financial partner.

CRITICAL THINKING QUESTION:

Would you rather own 100% of your business and assume all of the risks, or own a smaller percentage and share it?

MILLIONAIRE RESOURCE:

Read: Other People's Money: The Real Business of Finance, by John Kay

CHAPTER 31

Study Your Mind

The greatest asset you'll ever own is your brain, and your job is to study it so you can maximize its potential. The human mind is the most complex computer known to man, and every brain is a little different. Your mind has the power to make you rich or poor, fit or fat, happy or miserable. It all starts with the six inches between your ears. If everyone had the same brain, life might be easier, but it would probably be boring. Imagine if everyone liked the same music, sports, movies, work, hobbies, and food? We would be like robots. Luckily, we are not robots, but a genetic mix of various tastes, likes, and pleasures. Some millionaires love to work with numbers, while others prefer words. Some are introverts that would rather work alone, and others are extroverts that thrive on interaction. The key is to uncover who *you* are, what you love to do, and why you love to do it. The most effective way to do this is to try as many things as possible to see which gives you the greatest satisfaction. A lot of activities will grab your attention, but only a few will grab your heart. Move toward those, because as a young person building an empire, loving what you do will be the only reward you reap in the early days. Very few people become overnight successes. It happens, but mostly in movies. In the real world of getting rich, it's up to you to choose the battlefield on which you will make your stand. Studying your mind for what motivates and excites you is a good place to start. Visit your local bookstore and see which sections of books you naturally gravitate towards. Don't worry about whether you can make money or not in that field. That comes later. For now, let your natural interests and passions become your guide. Choosing an occupation that gives you a sense of fulfillment is crucial to your success. It may be the single most important choice you ever make, and the answer is already in your mind waiting to be discovered.

QUOTE:

"The human mind is our fundamental resource"—John F. Kennedy

ACTION STEP:

Write down the three most powerful things you've learned about your own mind.

CRITICAL THINKING QUESTION:

Do you believe your mind has the power to make you rich?

MILLIONAIRE RESOURCE:

Read: How the Mind Works, by Steven Pinker

CHAPTER 32

Money is Not Evil

The masses have been brainwashed for years with beliefs, superstitions, and concepts designed to control them, but perhaps none as destructive as the idea that *money is evil.* The purveyors of this nonsense will clarify it by saying; "it's the *love* of money that is evil." Here's the truth: rich people love money, and few of them are evil. There are poor and middle-class people who are evil, too. Being evil is about mental illness, not money. Evil people belong in hospitals. If you're going to get rich, you're going to have to love the freedom, opportunity and security money offers, which is effectively, *the love of money.* How can you possibly work for something for years, when the odds of attaining it are stacked against you, without loving it? It's preposterous. Avoid this argument with the masses. This is profoundly rooted in the collective consciousness that it's impossible to have a serious conversation about it with the average person. Never fight a fight you can't win, and never start an argument you can't finish. Remember that this belief gives the masses an excuse for their financial failure, and few will be willing to surrender it. The pursuit of profits and the love of its rewards, both material and psychological, have been almost single handily responsible for the upward rise of mankind. People don't start businesses, invent things, and risk their money on investments to save the world. They do it for the fulfillment it gives them and the profits it produces. That's not a politically correct statement; it's just the truth. Remove the money motive from the producers in America, and it's no longer America. Over the past 240+ years, America has evolved into the most powerful country in the world thanks to innovations of our profit driven producers. That's a fact. Even people who hate America can't deny that it's the richest and most prosperous country on earth. Even though these facts are clear, expect many of your teachers, professors, coaches, clergy, friends, and family to challenge them. Resist the urge to prove them wrong. Instead, focus your mental energy on getting rich. If you want to save the world after you become a self-made millionaire, that's fine. Just save yourself, first.

QUOTE:

"So you think that money is the root of all evil, have you ever asked what is the root of all money?"—Ayn Rand

ACTION STEP:

List three popular, false beliefs about money.

CRITICAL THINKING QUESTION:

Do people in power want the masses to believe that money is evil to keep them poor and easy to control or is the love of money truly evil?

MILLIONAIRE RESOURCE:

Read: How to Get Rich: One Of The World's Greatest Entrepreneurs Shares His Secrets, by Felix Dennis

CHAPTER 33

The Streets Are Paved with Gold

Despite what you'll hear from the masses, there are more opportunities to become wealthy in the world today than at any time in history. Since the invention of the Internet, the entire planet is only one click away. Information that previously took decades to acquire now takes seconds. It's an amazing time to be alive, and as a teenager, the opportunities will only get bigger and better through the course of your lifetime. You're going to experience things previous generations couldn't even dream up. Contrary to what you read in the press, life is going to be better for you than it was for your parents. You'll hear the opposite from the masses because they see the world through the eyes of fear. When the masses see problems, the world class sees opportunity. Self-made millionaires, like you're going to be, don't see problems and get scared. They see problems and get excited because problems require solutions, and solutions can be created and sold. The heart of every hard earned fortune is solutions to problems, and the bigger the solution, the bigger the fortune. Build the habit, from today forward, of becoming acutely aware of the problems encountered by people and society. Problems are everywhere, and new ones are popping up every day. All you have to do is marry your interests, talents, and skills to specific problems that people will pay to solve, and you're rich. I'm not saying it's easy. If it were, everyone who understands capitalism would be rich. You didn't think making more money in a week than most people make in a year would be easy, did you? If you did, change that belief. The streets may be paved with gold, but you're going to have to fight for your share of it. I'm talking about having the discipline, focus, determination, and sustained concentration to stick to your wealth building goals and dreams for as long as it takes to make them a reality.

Most people don't have that level of mental toughness, or at least they never access it. But you're different. You're being groomed to become one of the great ones, and that includes knowing the fight you are in for.

QUOTE:

"Opportunity does not knock, it presents itself when you beat down the door" —Kyle Chandler

ACTION STEP:

Write down three major problems that you've observed in society, and three potential solutions.

CRITICAL THINKING QUESTION:

What problem would you be most passionate about solving?

MILLIONAIRE RESOURCE:

Read: Acres of Diamonds, by Russell H. Conwell

CHAPTER 34

Avoid Microwave Thinking

Before microwave ovens were invented, people who cooked expected the process to take hours. Now that everyone has a microwave, we expect our meals in minutes. This mindset has bled over into every aspect of our modern day culture, and its programmed people to expect instant results in everything. In more recent years, services such as Google have added to this societal disorder by placing information on everything at our fingertips. You no longer have to spend hours in the library looking for answers, because they're all in the devices we hold in our hands. The technology that created this instant result syndrome is a huge leap for humanity. However, the syndrome that was created by it is not. Here's the bottom line: your financial empire will not be fortified overnight. It's going to take years to find the specific solutions to problems that will produce riches. You may fail dozens of times before you find your sweet spot to succeed. Most millionaires do. The trial and error process wipes out most would-be successful people after the first couple of failures. They lose money, fail at a solution, go bankrupt or suffer some other set back, and it's all over. They close up shop and crawl back to their old life with their proverbial tail between their legs. They whine about the work required to be in business, and how you have to be born rich to *become* rich. They expected to win the war overnight, and that rarely happens. If you're going to start a war, you'd better be willing to spend years on the battlefield before firing the first shot. Microwave thinking is for want-to-bees, and that's not you. Do your research, pick your problem and the solution you'll provide, and then attack it as though your life depended on it. Expect the fight to go all 15 rounds, and exhaust every idea you have to win. If you succeed, you're on your way to wealth. If you fail, use what you've learned as intellectual capital to begin again, more intelligently.

QUOTE:

"Don't exchange what you want most for what you want at the moment."

ACTION STEP:

Write down what are you willing to give up now that will help you get what you want later?

CRITICAL THINKING QUESTION:

What achievement in your life required the most discipline and delayed gratification?

MILLIONAIRE RESOURCE:

Read: The Willpower Instinct: How Self Control Works, Why It Matters, And What You Can Do To Get More Of It, by Kelly McGonigal, Ph.D.

CHAPTER 35

Dream Big

Most people stop dreaming after they spend a few years in the workplace. Life beats them down, and they never get up. You won't see this with millionaires. The self-made rich are the biggest dreamers in the world. They fearlessly and tirelessly take on risk and believe all of their ideas are winners. Of course, they're *not* all winners, but that doesn't discourage them. To the contrary, failure seems to make them fight harder to prove to themselves, and to the world, that they are right and deserve to be rich. They are the business equivalent of the Navy SEALs, and no one wants to go to up against them. Millionaires *must* dream. It's part of the world-class mindset. The question is, how *big* do you dream? At what point is the dream so big and seemingly far away that it no longer motivates you? This is a critical question in the formula of success. The answer is to dream as big as you can believe, and once you achieve that dream, expand it. Becoming a billionaire is a great dream, but dream of becoming a millionaire first. The masses love to talk about dreaming big, but few of them really understand it. How do we know this? Because very few of them live their dreams, and part of the reason they fail begins in the planning stage. Dreams are serious business, and if you don't understand the process, it won't serve you. If you walk up to 100 people on the street in New York City and ask them what their dream is, only 3-5 will have a serious answer. This is one of the fundamental reasons why the masses struggle. If you don't know what you want, how are you going to formulate a plan to get it? Start thinking about what you want out of your life, even if you're very young. You can always change your mind, but you want to build the habit of thinking about what motivates, excites and drives you. This will give you an edge over the other kids. This process is more important than any school you will ever attend. You're molding your mind to become a money machine, and dreaming big is where it all begins.

QUOTE:

"It's a funny thing about life, if you refuse to accept anything but the best, you very often get it." –W. Somerset Maugham

ACTION STEP:

Write down the three biggest dreams you have in life.

CRITICAL THINKING QUESTION:

Who is your favorite and most successful dreamer?

MILLIONAIRE RESOURCE:

Read: The Magic of Thinking Big, by David J. Schwartz, Ph.D.

CHAPTER 36

The Masses Are Sheep

Most people are passive followers. They believe everything they read and follow anyone with a loud enough voice or a lot of letters after their name. Don't get me wrong: average people are nice, caring and loving. Some of your best friends may be average people. And there's nothing wrong with being average—*unless you want to be rich.* Then you have to avoid their level of thinking like the plaque, and be careful how much exposure you have to them. I write and speak about this because it's my mission, but I don't recommend that you discuss this concept in mixed company. When you publicly expose the truth about people, they tend to dislike it, and they will attack you. It's not a battle you need to fight. I just want you to know that this is the way it is, and it's probably never going to change. In a way, it's a good thing, because it eliminates the majority of what would be your competition. Imagine how difficult it would be to succeed if everyone thought like a millionaire? In reality, only a tiny percentage of the population is made up of ambitious leaders who think for themselves. The winner's challenge conventional wisdom when they believe it's wrong, and sometimes the masses come after them. All of societies rules, laws and standards were made up by men no smarter than the average person. Thousands of years ago, people in power discovered that they could control the masses through fear, and that continues today. The only true power government leaders have is to make laws and wait for people to break them. So the average person quietly follows the laws, regulations and social constructs that keep them at the mercy of the people who created them. Once you know this, your job is to avoid following ideas, concepts, philosophies and behaviors you don't believe in. Don't be afraid. Be a leader and challenge what you think wrong. Make sure to protest or speak out within the rules of law. Don't be naïve enough to believe that sitting in a jail cell makes you a hero. It doesn't, it only makes you a criminal. Be smart and stick to the guidelines of the law, so your voice will be heard.

Sometimes you'll discover you're wrong, and other times, you'll be right. The point is to build the habit of thinking for yourself and not blindly following people just because they occupy positions of authority.

QUOTE:

"Do not go gentle into that good night. Rage, rage against the dying of the light." —Dylan Thomas

ACTION STEP:

Discuss one aspect of school that you think is wrong, unfair or sub standard with your parents.

CRITICAL THINKING QUESTION:

Are you willing to endure the criticism that comes along with challenging conventional wisdom?

MILLIONAIRE RESOURCE:

Read: 177 Mental Toughness Secrets of the World Class, by Steve Siebold

CHAPTER 37

Wealth is Nonlinear

School is going to teach you how to think in linear terms, in a straight line. 123. ABC. Unfortunately, the serious challenges in society are rarely solved at this basic level of thought. Nonlinear thinking, which means thinking in ways that are not as obvious or straightforward, is usually responsible for resolving the world's most complex problems. An example might be a bully you encounter at school. He's big, mean, and he steals your lunch money every day. The linear solution would be to tell him to stop it. That should work, right? Of course, it wouldn't. If it were that easy, millions of school children wouldn't be bullied every day. Another linear solution is to fight back. If you're big enough, this might work, but it's probably going to hurt. An even more popular linear solution adults like to offer is to squeal on the bully. Go to your teacher or the school Principal and get the bully in trouble. This works in theory, but you and I both know that he's going to find you off of school grounds where the teachers can't protect you. A nonlinear solution has nothing to do with squealing or fighting, but it will stop him. It's called gaining leverage, and it means you're going to create a reason for this bully to stop picking on you. Now, if you're thinking that this is not going to be easy, you're correct. Nonlinear thinking is the highest and most difficult level of thought because it's so abstract. The first step is to study the bully. Ask people whom he is, where he comes from, what he cares about and what his weaknesses are. The odds are that you're not his first victim, and other kids will be willing to share, especially if you can help them. Due to the nature of nonlinear thought, the possible solutions to gain leverage on your bully are endless, so I'll give you my own example. In high school, I dated a girl that was the former girlfriend of a guy in a gang. He found out I was dating her and threatened to hurt me. He was mean and nasty, so fighting back was not going to work. Over the course of a few days, I asked a lot of questions about him, and it turned out that the only guy in the school my bully feared was the middle linebacker for our football team, with whom I was on good terms. So I approached the linebacker and asked him what I would need to do for him in exchange for getting this monster off my back? He said, "I've been trying to date the head cheerleader all year, and she won't even give me her phone number. If you can get her number and convince her to take my call, I'll handle this bonehead for you." I got her number, he took her to the prom, and without anyone throwing a single punch, and the bully never bothered me again. To this day, I don't know what the linebacker said, nor do I care. The result was everyone got what they wanted, and no one got hurt. That's what it means to gain leverage, and it begins with nonlinear thinking. Most wealth is acquired the same way; by using nonlinear thought to solve problems in ways no one has thought about before, and the reason they've never considered these solutions is that they were thinking in simple, linear terms.

QUOTE:

"Creating linear solutions will make you a living. Creating nonlinear solutions will make you rich."

ACTION STEP:

Try to think of a time in your life that you used nonlinear thinking to solve a problem.

CRITICAL THINKING QUESTION:

What is a linear vs. a nonlinear solution to getting better grades in school?

MILLIONAIRE RESOURCE:

Read: Wealth: Is It Worth It?, by S. Truett Cathy

CHAPTER 38

Money is Meaningless

You're going love being rich. It's fabulous. Anyone that tells you otherwise has never experienced it. Many people that have never had money assume they know what it's like, but they don't. Waking up every day with millions of dollars in the bank is an amazing feeling, mostly because you don't have to worry about it. For Americans and others like us fortunate enough to live in wealthy countries, being rich is like having more food than you need. It doesn't guarantee your happiness, but it's certainly a foundation on which to build. If your parents purchased this book and they're studying it with you, chances are you've never had to worry about your next meal. The sad fact is that billions of people around the globe are food insecure. This means the main focus of their life is escaping starvation. As I said in an earlier chapter, the world is a beautiful and brutal place. My point of this parallel is that being rich is equivalent to being food secure, except with money. When you're food secure and hungry, you go to the kitchen and eat. When you're rich, and you need money, you go to the bank get money. After a while, you rarely give it much thought, because there's always more than enough, so why waste your time thinking about it? That's where being wealthy begins and ends. It has no meaning other than that. Granted, being rich and never having to worry about money is a big deal, but it doesn't mean more than the lack of worrying about. Being rich doesn't mean you're any smarter, savvier or superior to anyone else. It just means you're rich. If you adopt this philosophy, it will keep you grounded and prevent you from buying into the hero worship the masses have for the wealthy. Being rich doesn't make you a hero, so be careful not to believe your own press.

There's an ancient piece of wisdom to explain how to handle praise and adulation: "smell the perfume, but never drink it."

QUOTE:

"After a certain point, money is meaningless. It ceases to be the goal. The game is what counts." —Aristotle Onassis

ACTION STEP:

Just for today, notice how often you worry about food.

CRITICAL THINKING QUESTION:

Can you imagine living your life without ever worrying or thinking about money?

MILLIONAIRE RESOURCE:

Read: The Teen Money Manual: A Guide To Cash, Credit, Spending, Saving, Wealth, Work and More, by Kara McGuire

CHAPTER 39

Spend Smart

You're going to be rich, but no matter how rich you are, excessive spending can ruin you. It happens every day to people with millions of dollars at their disposal. Spending money is easy to do, no matter how much you have. There's an old saying you'll want to adopt: live below your means. Everyone gets a charge out of showing off their success, especially after years of people doubting and discouraging you. You might expect me to tell you not to indulge in this, but I won't, because taking a couple of victory laps after years of struggling is not only fun, it's also *well deserved.* Just make sure you don't overextend yourself in the process because that will put you on a treadmill of having and not having money. A lot of new rich people do this, and it's exhausting. If you're like Warren Buffet and you prefer to live frugally, then do it. That's the safest way to ensure you never have a spending problem. But if you're like most people, including me, you don't want to live in the house you grew up in, and you don't want to drive around in your fathers Oldsmobile. You may feel like you've earned the right to live a life a luxury, and you'll be right. If your dream is to drive a red Ferrari, and you can afford it, drive it. If you want to live in a mansion and it's not going to break you, build it. If you want a private jet, and it's not going to put a dent in your bank account, buy it. Just remember what it took to get you where you are today, and you don't want to lose it. If you do the math, and you want some or all of those things, but can't really afford them, set a goal to acquire the money you need, and *then* buy them. When you're rich, people rarely tell you what to do. You need to discipline *yourself* and protect the wealth you've built. It doesn't mean you can't have a blast buying what you want, but you may have to wait until you're a little richer to truly afford it. Treat it like a game, and you'll enjoy the process while never jeopardizing the wealth you've worked so hard to create.

QUOTE:

"We often overspend because we are trying to fill an emotional gap in our lives. No object will ever satisfy your soul"—Dave Ramsey

ACTION STEP:

Begin building your personal library of books on money.

CRITICAL THINKING QUESTION:

If you were to invest in your future by reading three books on money each year, how far ahead of your peers would you be in this area by the time you entered college?

MILLIONAIRE RESOURCE:

Read: OMG: Official Money Guide for Teenagers, by Susan P. Beacham and Michael P. Beacham

CHAPTER 40

Get Mentally Tough

One of the requirements of getting rich is becoming mentally tough. This means becoming a master at controlling and manipulating your emotions to serve your best interests. As you're building your empire, people are going to attempt to derail your efforts by discouraging you, and you'll have to be mentally tough enough to take it. You're going to have multiple failures along the way, and only mental toughness will keep you coming back. At some point in your ascent to greatness, you'll doubt yourself and wonder if this is all just a pipedream. Mental toughness will calm your fears and reassure you that you're on the right track. You're likely to have problems with partners, disagreements with banks, and trouble with products and services. Mental toughness will keep you in the ring until the battle is won. Mental toughness won't solve every problem you'll encounter on the road to wealth, but it will solve 90% of them. It's a big deal, and that's why I want you to *master* it. The first step is deciding on whatever goals and dreams you wish to accomplish, and that you will do whatever it takes to persist until you succeed. It sounds easy until life throws you to the floor, and then it gets real. Building wealth can drive you to a level of frustration that's unimaginable to the masses. It can cause toxic levels of stress and keep you up at night. It's all part of the process, and the most twisted part of it is, *this is what makes you mentally tough.* See, you don't get mentally tough by reading a book, listening to a speech or attending a seminar. Those kinds of resources give you tools to help you navigate the storm, but only the storm itself will make you mentally tough. It's a decision you make to win, regardless of the pain you must endure. And this decision must be made before you know how much suffering is going to be necessary. While anyone is capable of becoming mentally tough, most people rely on mind-altering substances like alcohol, food, and drugs to numb the pain. Some people have serious psychological issues and are forced to rely on prescription medication, but I'm not referring to them. I'm talking about the 99% of us who don't want to face the fight. While there's nothing inherently wrong with this, as a person being groomed to be rich, it's not for you. Instead, mental toughness is the answer, and it will help you thrive through all the challenges that life presents.

QUOTE:

"Mental toughness is when you find fuel in an empty tank."

ACTION STEP:

List three things that you'd love to do, but you're afraid to do.

CRITICAL THINKING QUESTION:

Would doing something you're afraid to do today make you more mentally tough tomorrow?

MILLIONAIRE RESOURCE:

Read: As A Man Thinketh, by James Allen

CHAPTER 41

Give

The mass consciousness is famous for believing that rich people must practice altruism. The premise is that we are all our brother's keeper, and if we become successful, we are morally bound to give part of our fortune to charity. While giving is a nice idea, the belief that the rich are immoral if they refuse to surrender their silver, is ludicrous. I'm not suggesting, that once you get rich, you shouldn't help others I'm simply saying you are not *obligated* to do so. It's your money, and as a result, your choice. It's that simple. Be prepared to hear the opposite from teachers, coaches, clergy and other adults. Remember that most people don't think for themselves, they just repeat what they're taught and pass it down to the next generation. Most of them have never struggled for years to build a financial empire. They prefer that you do the work and give them your money. And I'm not exaggerating. Washington, DC is packed with people who are running our country, and many of them believe if you're rich, you just got lucky and should share your bounty. Where were these people when you were working 16-hour days? Probably out with friends, playing softball or gaming until 3am. And now you're expected to support them? Believe it or not, yes. Or so many people say. Be on the look out for people attempting to guilt you into giving. That being said, if you decide to share your success because you want to, the chances are that *you* will be the biggest beneficiary. Giving to someone in need, or cause you care about is a spiritual experience. There are so many people struggling that the difficult part is pinpointing who or what organization to give to. You also have to research the organizations you support, because wherever you'll find tax-free donations, you'll find corruption. You might be wondering how leaders of charitable organizations could cheat the very people they're supposed to be helping? It's a good question, and the answer is greed. It's a low level of consciousness rooted in fear, and believe it or not, it's common among charities. Deciding what legitimate organizations to support is a business in itself, but if you're going to give, do your homework, so the money goes to the people who need it instead of corrupt leaders.

QUOTE:

"Don't give back, just give"—Dr. Nido Qubein

ACTION STEP:

Give a small donation, even a dollar, to a charity, cause or person of your choice and notice how it makes you feel.

CRITICAL THINKING QUESTION:

How do you believe giving will make you feel?

MILLIONAIRE RESOURCE:

Read: The Giving Way To Happiness, by Jenny Santi

CHAPTER 42

You Deserve To Be Rich

In a free market economy like America, if you serve enough people and solve enough problems, you deserve to be rich. The marketplace rewards people on performance, not promises. A lot of business people talk a good game, but only the best deliver. Study the most successful self-made millionaires, and you'll find a substantial trail of satisfied customers. This is capitalism at its best, but don't expect the average person to believe it. Even in America, the richest country in the history of the world, a large percentage of the population passionately opposes this idea. They believe that you can only be rich if you were born into the right family, attended the best school or possess exceptional talent. While these advantages certainly help, they are by no means required to be rich. Often time's people from upper-class families and Ivy League pedigree never develop the hunger it takes to build a business or career. Some are spoiled from years of easy living, and they often end up with mediocre accomplishments. Show me an entrepreneur with fire in his eyes and the mental toughness to persist in the face of failure, and I'll show you a future millionaire that deserves every penny he earns. The only people who tell you that the self-made rich don't deserve it are people that have never done it. Believe me, by the time you get rich, you'll be convinced that you've earned it. But don't expect the masses to agree, no matter how hard you work or how much service you provide. It's wise to factor in the role that jealousy plays. The fact is that most people don't have the ambition or the guts to go out and stake their claim, and when *you* do, they get jealous. Your success becomes a mirror, and when they look, they don't like what they see. It's easier to demonize the rich than it is to become one of them. You served the market place, and it made you rich. That's what built America. It's the producers, not the jealous critics that earn the right to be rich.

QUOTE:

"The best way to get what you want is to deserve what you want"—Charlie Munger

ACTION STEP:

Open a savings account and begin making small deposits

CRITICAL THINKING QUESTION:

What actions would you need to take in the future that would make you feel like you deserved to be rich?

MILLIONAIRE RESOURCE:

Read: Focal Point, by Brian Tracy

CHAPTER 43

Be Optimistic and Pessimistic

You're going to hear a lot about the positive thinking, and how optimism is better than pessimism. And while there's merit in this idea, building a fortune cannot be reduced to such simplicity. Sometimes negative thinking will save you from hiring the wrong people, making poor investments or taking too big of risks. There's value in looking at potential downsides of your decisions because sometimes passing up an opportunity is the smartest strategy. The same stands true for optimism, which is almost a prerequisite for large-scale success, yet sometimes pessimism is more prudent. Every self-made millionaire has dozens of stories of how being pessimistic saved him from a financial catastrophe. The average business person focuses on the upside of a deal, and sometimes their optimism blinds them to the dangers of the downside. They want to believe so badly that they often ignore the warning signs. The upside of a deal is simple, because benefits take care of themselves. You don't need to manage the upside of a deal, but you *must* manage the downside. Invest the majority of your time looking for potential pitfalls and problems. Create hypothetical, worst case scenarios for every deal and put them on paper. Dissect every detail for flaws and hidden threats. Once you have written this out, weigh the benefits against the risks. And then ask yourself these critical thinking questions: 1. Can I recover if these threats are realized? 2. Is the potential benefit worth the risk? 3. How disruptive is this deal going to be in my business? You're better served to be more of a pessimist in business than an optimist. It's not as much fun, but it's more prudent. Be more optimistic in your personal life, where the potential repercussions are less severe.

QUOTE:

"I'm a pessimist because of intelligence, but I'm an optimist because of will"—Antonio Gramsci

ACTION STEP:

Would you say your parents are more optimistic or pessimistic?

CRITICAL THINKING QUESTION:

Why is pessimism important in business?

MILLIONAIRE RESOURCE:

Read: Learned Optimism: How To Change Your Mind and Your Life, by Dr. Martin Seligman

CHAPTER 44

Make Your Mark

One of the things you'll need to consider is how will you make your mark. In other words, what benefit will you leave the world? There are many ways to get rich, and your job is to decide how you want to do it. The secret is to select a field you love, combine it with your talent, and determine if it has enough profit potential. This is a Herculean task and may require years of soul searching and market analysis. No matter how long it takes, it *must* be done. The key is to make the correct selection the first time, so you don't waste years pursuing the wrong field. Many entrepreneurs jump too fast and end up changing careers multiple times. As young as you are now when you become an adult time seems to move faster, and you only have limited time to make your mark. So work hard on thinking of your field of choice and carefully evaluate each potential profession as if your life depended on it. Be prepared to hear guidance counselors, in high school and college, advising you to study fields where your grades are highest, and opportunities are most abundant. This isn't bad advice, but it's typical of the mass consciousness. If you get high grades in math, but bad grades in English, does it mean you should eliminate every field that involves English? No, because everything in business boils down to numbers. Just because you failed English doesn't mean you can't specialize in a related field. You may have failed because you didn't pay attention or didn't like the teacher. My point is to be aware of pedestrian, simple-minded advice that fails to factor in all variables in the equation. This decision is a big deal, and the truth is that most people get it wrong. They simply go with the flow and follow the easiest path they can find. Millionaires don't do this. They discipline themselves to dissect every detail, and they have the confidence that they'll eventually arrive at the right decision. Once you decide on what field in which you will build your expertise, the next step is to decide what you will bring to the market place that will be different, unique and valuable to people. That's how you make your mark. Vinton Cerf, the engineer from MCI, may have created the first email message, but Bill Gates brought it to the masses. IBM made their mark building super computers, and Steve Jobs created a user-friendly model for the masses. These people and companies worked in the same field, but they all made their mark by adding value in their own unique way.

QUOTE:

"Making your mark on the world is hard. If it were easy, everybody would do it. But it's not. It takes patience, it takes commitment, and it comes with plenty of failures along the way."—Barack Obama

ACTION STEP:

Make of list of your 10 favorite things to do.

CRITICAL THINKING QUESTION:

Does anyone make a living doing any of your 10 favorite things?

MILLIONAIRE RESOURCE:

Read: Finding Your Element: How To Discover Your Talents and Passions and Transform Your Life, by Ken Robinson, Ph.D. and Lou Aronica

CHAPTER 45

Money is Infinite

You're going to be bombarded with false axioms about money, the majority of which will scream of how scarce it is. "Money doesn't grow on trees" is an example. While money doesn't literally grow on trees, this Axiom's goal to point out how *difficult* it is to make money. The fact is that earning money in a free market economy is *no*t difficult. You simply have to supply a product or service that's in demand. Every Girl Scout in America knows that people love cookies, and they sell millions of them every year. Think of it this way: if a ten-year old girl can earn solid profits selling cookies how difficult can it be? The background of this axiom comes from the masses that go to work every day and provide little value to their employer. And if you're providing little value, it's next to impossible to earn big money. This has nothing to do with money, and everything to do with how much value the average person provides. While money, as a commodity, is finite, the potential to transfer more of it from the customer's bank account to yours, is infinite. Think of it this way: if earning money is based on solving problems, and the number of problems is infinite, then your ability to earn money is infinite. The point of this is to reject the mass belief that money is a scarce resource, like some endangered animal in the jungle. It's not. What is scarce are people with solutions that others want to buy, and *that's* what you need to master. Once you create your first solution and profit from it, you'll see how simple the process is, and you'll begin searching for the next solution. Some of your solutions will sell, and others will fall flat, but that's how capitalism works. When you succeed, you profit, and when you fail, you learn from your mistakes and use that education to create your next solution.

QUOTE:

"Money flows like water to good ideas."

ACTION STEP:

Ask three people if earning money is easy.

CRITICAL THINKING QUESTION:

Does believing that earning money is easy serve your best interests?

MILLIONAIRE RESOURCE:

Read: The 100 Most Powerful Affirmations of the Rich, by Jason Thomas

CHAPTER 46

You're Not Entitled

The world owes you nothing. No one is entitled to anything. It's up to you to create your own future. The idea of entitlement seems to be growing in popularity, yet it's based on the delusion that we are born with certain rights. We're not. We're just born. The rest is up to you. The good news is that people who get something for nothing usually don't appreciate it, and it robs them of the exhilaration of the experience. Parents that turn over large sums of money to their kids are actually behaving selfishly. Giving their kids money, buying them fancy cars and lavish gifts, make parents feel like they've succeeded. It makes them feel important, and it's bad parenting. As a teenager being groomed for greatness, you need to abandon any thoughts of entitlement and getting something for nothing. In the education you're getting on being rich, you're not going to need charity. Refuse to take shortcuts in your success, because all it will do is lengthen the process. Focus your thoughts on creating solutions to problems. Donald Trump has spent his entire adult life denying that the money his father gave him to fund his business is what made him successful. He claims he could have succeeded without the money. The truth is he'll never know, and it's obvious that it bothers him when people bring this to his attention. If you ask for help, be sure to bring value in exchange. Never expect something for nothing. This way you'll never have to defend your success to the world. The opposite of the entitled mentality is self-reliance, and this is the philosophy you'll want to adopt. The irony of this is that the more you exhibit your self-reliant attitude; the more people want to help you.

QUOTE:

"Don't feel entitled to anything you didn't sweat and struggle for" —Marian Wright Edelman

ACTION STEP:

List three things you are most grateful for?

CRITICAL THINKING QUESTION:

Do you believe that gratitude eliminates entitlement?

MILLIONAIRE RESOURCE:

Read: The Entitlement Cure: Finding Success in Doing Hard Things The Right Way, by Dr. John Townsend

CHAPTER 47

Embrace Your Ambition

Never apologize for wanting to be rich. If you proclaim it publicly, expect to be criticized. Even in America, where we idolize success, speaking about it openly will draw fire. If you're wondering how this makes sense, your guess is as good as mine. It doesn't, but that's the way it is. The irony here is that in a free market, you're either rich or you work for someone or some organization that is. What if there were no rich people or rich corporations with the money to employ people? What would the masses do? How would they earn a living? You would think that publicly declaring your ambition to be rich would win you favor, but it rarely happens. The masses want to denigrate the producers while simultaneously hoping they will hire them. It's equivalent to biting the hand that feeds you. Do not allow this low level of consciousness to erode your ambition or make you feel guilty. Ambitious people who provide employment for everyone else built America. As you engage your ambition, you become part of a special group of people with the courage to face the world fearlessly. All of the greatest innovations, inventions, and creations start with an ambitious person with a dream. People criticize them, too, so you're in good company. Without ambitious people, America wouldn't exist. So be proud of your desire to be successful and rich, and be grateful that you have the opportunity to make it happen. If people accuse you of being self-centered or shallow, tell them you believe in self-reliance. And if they continue to attack you, walk away. Keep in mind that the mass consciousness is always going to be there, and it's futile to fight them. Just go to work and make your dreams reality.

QUOTE:

"Ambition beats genius 99% of the time." —Jay Leno

ACTION STEP:

List your three biggest ambitions.

CRITICAL THINKING QUESTION:

Is it possible to strengthen your ambitions?

MILLIONAIRE RESOURCE:

Read: Ambition and Success, by Orison Swett Marden

CHAPTER 48

Broaden Your Worldview

The world is a big place. The more you explore it, the more accurate your representation of it will become. America, with all of our success, power, and prestige, is a polarizing nation that appears to lead the rest of civilization in almost every area. Deeper exploration shows that this is not entirely true. Yes, America is a great country in many ways. In other ways, we are not the best, and we can learn from other countries and cultures, most of which have been around a lot longer. Take the tiny country of Costa Rica: It's a tropical rainforest located in Latin America with a population of 4 million people. Their biggest income sources are tourism, coffee, and bananas. Costa Rica is a not a rich country. The average Costa Rican earns around $10,000 US dollars per year. Yet, in the World Happiness Report, they rank #12 in the world out of 155 countries, while the United States ranks #14. So what is it that these poor people have figured out about happiness that we haven't? In America, we have every modern convenience known to man, whereas the average Costa Rican doesn't even have air conditioning. Americans are among the most highly stressed people in the world, and Costa Ricans are among the lowest. What have they learned about living peacefully that we haven't? Now cross over the pond, to France, where the average workweek is a fraction of ours, yet their productivity remains high. The French place a high value on the arts, whereas in America, we're cutting them out of our schools. Now slide down under to Australia, where you'll meet some of the friendliest people on the planet. The Aussies don't seem interested in quarreling with anyone, and they've found a way to enjoy life beyond stress and struggle. These are just a few examples of countries and cultures from which you can learn. The more you travel, the broader your worldview becomes. You can read about these places in books, but nothing replaces the impact of traveling to them and meeting their people. It's an education that's impossible to acquire in any other way.

QUOTE:

"The more you see, the more you understand."

ACTION STEP:

List three countries you would like to visit.

CRITICAL THINKING QUESTION:

Would visiting these three countries help to broaden your worldview?

MILLIONAIRE RESOURCE:

Read: What's Your Worldview, by James N. Anderson

CHAPTER 49

Play Rich Sports

Rich people play rich sports. Golf and Tennis are among the richest. In America, football is the most popular, but the brain is not equipped to handle the blunt force trauma that the sport requires. Football is a great game, but it's not a sport of the rich and it's too dangerous to play. Multiple concussions won't help you think at a higher level. Golf is the most popular sport of the rich, and I highly recommend that you give it a try. Take some lessons and see if you enjoy it, and if not, try tennis. You don't have to be rich to play tennis, but a lot of rich people play. You want to play rich sports so you can associate with rich people. Sports allow you to meet and interact with them in a non-threatening way. More deals are done on golf courses than in boardrooms. Now I'll be honest: I hate golf. I tried it, took lessons, and played on beautiful courses from Palm Beach to Palm Springs. I still hate it. It's slow and boring. Early in my golf experience, I met many top business people. Almost everyone I met was a senior executive in a corporation, a successful entrepreneur or a tenured professional. I quit playing golf after 6 months, but I never left the game completely. The potential business was just too alluring. In the past 20 years, I've joined three world-class golf clubs and purchased millions of dollars in property on golf courses. As a result, I get invited to the neighborhood golf parties and other functions and landed millions of dollars in deals with the golfers I've met. Tennis is a distant number two, but it's also a sport rich people enjoy. As a former professional tennis player, I've used my tennis skills to meet a lot of people I wouldn't have met in any other way. Sports like baseball, soccer, wrestling, gymnastics, and basketball are all wonderful. Rich people watch them, but they usually don't play them. If you love one of these sports, play them for fun and exercise. But when it comes to positioning yourself to succeed, find a way to incorporate tennis and golf into your life.

QUOTE:

"Golf is like a 6-hour sales call"—Bill Storer

ACTION STEP:

Take a golf lesson and see if you like it.

CRITICAL THINKING QUESTION:

Is it possible to use golf, tennis or another sport of the wealthy as a nonlinear business strategy?

MILLIONAIRE RESOURCE:

Read: Selling on the Green: The Art of Building Trusted Relationships and Growing Your Business on The Golf Course, by Jonathan Taylor and Tim Davis

CHAPTER 50

Don't Get Fat

Staying fit is a healthy way to live, and it shows the world what you think of yourself. This doesn't mean you have to become a body builder or compete in triathlons, just that you should maintain a healthy physique through regular exercise and a nutritionally sound diet. In 2018 America, according to the Centers for Disease Control, (CDC), 40% of women and 35% of men are considered obese, and nearly 70% of all Americans are overweight. It's getting worse every year, and the trend will most likely continue. These sad statistics have dire consequences, as obesity contributes to almost every major disease. That's the bad news. The good news is this creates an opportunity for you to separate yourself from the masses in the minds of people who can help you. Let's face it: when 70% of the population is fat, the fit person looks like Super Man or Wonder Woman. Your fitness will draw attention to your success in this area. As an upcoming millionaire, your level of fitness shows your teachers, coaches, friends, and family how much respect you have for your body, and for yourself. It exhibits your level of discipline and self-control. Your fitness is a showcase for the way you think because thinking is where fitness begins. The two most important steps you can take are healthy eating and robust exercise. Skip the pizza parties and avoid sitting on the couch playing video games. When it comes to achieving world-class success, remember that everything affects everything. In other words, every action you take has an impact on every other action. When you eat right, you'll be motivated to exercise. When you're exercising regularly, you'll want to eat right. When you look and feel good, you'll want to do more of both.

QUOTE:

"Exercise is king and diet is queen"—Jack Lalane

ACTION STEP:

Start a regular exercise program and healthy diet regimen.

CRITICAL THINKING QUESTION:

Can your level of fitness impact your success and happiness in life?

MILLIONAIRE RESOURCE:

Fat Loser: Mental Toughness Training for Dieters, by Steve Siebold

CHAPTER 51

Be Visionary

As a future millionaire, you need to be able to see the future long before it arrives. In other words, you have to know what you want, why you want it and what you're willing to sacrifice to get it. The average person takes life as it comes, with little concern for long term planning. It's enough for most people to live day by day and see what develops. They go with the wind, and change direction when the road gets rough. Not you. You're being groomed to be rich, and that means following the vision you have set for yourself. You must see the vision years in advance and be willing to adapt it as you grow. Let's say you create a written vision at age 13 to make your first million by age 25. At age 30, you cash in and retire to an island in the Caribbean. You see yourself paddle boarding every day through the warm, blue-green waters and relaxing on the beach. Sounds good, right? But...by age 15, you're no longer interested in paddle boarding, so you remove that from your vision. You decide you'd rather retire in Aspen after your parents took you there last Christmas. So you change the vision to meet your current passions, interests, and dreams. Being visionary doesn't mean being static, it means being focused on the future and being able to see, taste and touch it as if it were real. Your vision is a living, breathing document that should change and grow as you evolve. Some dreams you envision will be changed or eliminated quickly, and others may be there for 50 years. The truth is it doesn't really matter, as long as you identify what you want out of your life and adjust it as you evolve. Being visionary keeps you focused on where you're going and eliminates procrastination in performance and hesitation in decision-making. It's a big deal. Start your written vision today by making a list of what you want to be, have and do in your life. After that, write a letter to a friend addressed to the future date in which you've decided to achieve these things. Write the letter as if all of these things have come true and tell your friend what it feels like to be on top of the mountain. This is your first step to becoming a true visionary.

QUOTE:

"Man creates the vision, and then the vision creates the man."

ACTION STEP:

Write a letter to a friend in which you describe the life you wish to live 10 years in the future; and write it in the present tense, as if it's already happened.

CRITICAL THINKING QUESTION:

Have you started to consider what you really want out of life?

MILLIONAIRE RESOURCE:

Read: What Do You Really Want? How to Set a Goal and Go For It! A Guide For Teens, by Beverly K. Bachel

CHAPTER 52

Cocoon Yourself

As a future world-class performer, you're going to need to be selective over who gains access to your inner circle. The masses can hang around anyone, but you don't have that luxury. The people you associate with will influence your thinking and decision making, even if it occurs subconsciously. This means you have to carefully select the people for which you spend any substantial amount of time. It also means cocooning yourself. In other words, creating a cocoon around you that keeps people away that do not serve your long-term best interests. This is what many professional sports coaches do with athletes to assist them in maintaining the world-class mindset that makes them great. As you might expect, this is going to infuriate people who are blocked by your cocoon. Just remember that most people have no idea as to the level of preparation, discipline and focus it takes to get rich.

The masses see cocooning as an elitist action successful people take to isolate themselves from others because they think they're better. Not true. Cocooning is about protecting your consciousness from the fear and scarcity based mindset that plagues the masses. Over 100 years ago, Albert Einstein described this phenomenon perfectly when he said; "Consciousness is contagious." Dr. Einstein couldn't have been more right, and it can work for or against you, depending on the level of consciousness in which the people you allow into your inner circle are operating. Your job, from this day forward, is to cultivate relationships with the brightest kids in your classes and in your neighborhood. Maybe you feel more connected to the cool kids that play on the football team and sit in the back of the class. Get over it. The smart kids sit in the front row, and that's where you need to be. Hopefully, you'll enjoy your new environment. If not, consider it part of the sacrifice of getting rich. If this sounds extreme, I understand where you're coming from, because I used to feel the same way, back when I was broke. After I took this same advice from a billionaire many years ago, I came to realize how crucial this strategy is. I complained to the billionaire that this was too radical, but I still did it. Then I got rich, and I stopped complaining. You know what you have to do. Now go do it.

QUOTE:

"You'll be the average of the 5 people you spend the most time with" —Jim Rohn

ACTION STEP:

Start sitting in the front of the class.

CRITICAL THINKING QUESTION:

How have your best friends impacted your behavior?

MILLIONAIRE RESOURCE:

Read: How to Win Friends and Influence People, by Dale Carnegie

CHAPTER 53

Manage Your Money

You are going to have a lot of money, and you're going to have to learn to manage it. Once you cover your expenses, what do you do with all that excess cash? Invest it in the stock market? Real estate? Silver and Gold? Hide it under your mattress? The answer depends on a number of variables, such as market conditions, your current portfolio, age, tolerance for risk and future goals. If it sounds difficult, that's because it is, and most people don't know where to start. A percentage of people hire experts to manage their money, and that service can be valuable. Consider hiring a professional to *oversee* your money, but remember that it's your job to *manage* it. Even if you have a Wall Street hedge fund manager investing your money, it's your job to *manage your manager.* This is why you must learn everything you can about money and markets. And not just traditional markets, like the stock and bond markets. I'm talking about studying non-traditional markets where you can invest money, such as the fine arts, collectibles, vintage musical instruments, jewelry, antique automobiles, sports memorabilia, etc. These markets are no less tricky and volatile than their traditional counterparts, yet they often deliver similar returns with less risk. Becoming highly educated in the growth and management of money doesn't guarantee that you'll be successful, just ask the pros on Wall Street. Start studying during your teenage years, and by the time you get to start college, you'll be on your way to developing real expertise.

QUOTE:

"Be aware of the little expenses. A small leak will sink a great ship."—Ben Franklin

ACTION STEP:

Create a spend/save ratio with your allowance: spend 75% and save 25%.

CRITICAL THINKING QUESTION:

Are you willing to save today so you can have what you want tomorrow?

MILLIONAIRE RESOURCE:

Read: The Money Class: A Course in Basic Money Management for Teens and Young Adults, by Michael James Minyard

CHAPTER 54

Never Deny Luck

The masses will tell you there's no such thing as luck. You'll also hear that luck is simply opportunity combined with preparedness. As I've mentioned in previous chapters, there are hundreds of axioms the masses make up to help them make sense of the world, and they range from reasonably rational to downright ridiculous. This stems from the overwhelming fear they feel as they mature and attempt to reconcile a life of random events. Instead of growing up emotionally and embracing the harsh realities of life, they simply make up their own reasons that things happen to comfort themselves. The masses consciously choose to create their own fairy tales and build their lives around magical thinking. This is only possible because man is an emotional creature, and emotional beings can be brainwashed to believe almost anything, no matter how intelligent or educated they may be. Most of it's designed to calm the fears of a terrified species which are evolved enough to construct a nuclear bomb yet devolved enough to use it. The level of magical thinking you've been programmed with throughout your life will determine how offended you are at these statements. But as with all truths, time and careful consideration will make these things evident to you. For the average person willing to settle for a modest existence, I wouldn't even bring this up. Taking away the teddy bear that calms their fears in the night is unnecessary, and maybe even a little mean. But you are not the average person. You're going to be a self-made millionaire and live a lifestyle that only a fraction of people on the planet even know exists. And that means you don't have the luxury of living in a made up fantasy world. You don't build a millionaires life on a foundation of fairy tales. You must see the world as it is: wonderful and horrible. Amazing and disgusting; heroic and tragic; all at the same time. Here's the reality of luck: it can be good or bad, for no reason and without logic. Sometimes you get lucky, and other times you don't. Prepare for bad luck and be grateful for good luck. And don't waste time attempting to make sense of either.

QUOTE:

"You never know what worse luck your bad luck has saved you from" —Cormac McCarthy

ACTION STEP:

Start telling yourself every day that you are lucky.

CRITICAL THINKING QUESTION:

Do you believe it's possible to talk yourself into being lucky?

MILLIONAIRE RESOURCE:

Read: Strategies for Attracting Good Luck, by Gail Howard

CHAPTER 55

Take Calculated Risks

One of the misconceptions the masses have about self-made millionaires is that they are adrenaline addicted risk takers. This is not true. The ultra successful go to extraordinary lengths to mitigate risk and exposure. The rich don't *bet* on the ponies, they *own* the ponies. Instead of paving new roads of risk, they prefer to own the tollbooths. People who watch too many movies generally espouse the idea that the rich are gamblers. Gambling is a loser's game unless you're the house. That's why Las Vegas Boulevard is lined with some of the most expensive hotels in the world. The millions of people who party and gamble in Vegas built those hotels with their losses. In the real world, the house always wins. That's the mentality of millionaires. They want to *be the house.* Is building a world-class hotel on the Vegas strip a risk? Sure. But it's a calculated risk, based on years of data showing the costs and potential benefits. This is not the risk taking of an adrenaline junkie. That's the guy in the casino at Caesars Palace gambling away his 401K. Calculated risk taking requires extensive research, after which an assessment is made, and the true level of risk determined. Once the millionaire understands the risk, she moves to the next step of assessing the financial fall out if the risk fails. She pours over the numbers with her team of experts to determine if the enterprise could survive this level of failure. The larger the risk, the more time and assessment are required. Some of these deals take weeks, and others take years. Now does that sound anything like an irresponsible, adrenaline loving risk taker? It's quite the opposite, but the masses love to make the excuse that they're not rich because they have families and can't afford the gamble. You're going to hear this message from the masses your entire life, and it's one of many misconceptions that keep them struggling financially.

QUOTE:

"A ship is safe in harbor, but that's not what ships are made for." —William G.T. Shedd

ACTION STEP:

Ask someone you are attracted to out on a date.

CRITICAL THINKING QUESTION:

Do you believe that calculated risk taking is a skill that you develop through use?

MILLIONAIRE RESOURCE:

Read: Raising an Entrepreneur: 10 Rules for Nurturing Risk Takers, Problem Solvers and Change Makers, by Margot Machol Bisnow and Elliott Bisnow

CHAPTER 56

Security Doesn't Exist

Among the magical beliefs of the masses is the idea of financial security. While being rich is more secure than being poor, financial security is largely a mythical concept created by society to reduce fear. An extension of this myth is the idea that being employed by a large corporation offers you greater security than a small business, or by being in business for yourself. The fact is that the only true security any of us has lies in our ability to perform. Where or what size structure in which we choose to perform is mostly irrelevant, although a large corporation usually takes more time to terminate you. This is to prevent people from attempting to sue them. Big corporations invest millions, and sometimes billions of dollars, building huge human resource and legal departments to minimize the number of lawsuits filed by disgruntled employees. Once a manager decides to separate (fire) an employee from their team, it may take months to document the reasons and make a case for termination. That buys an employee a little extra time, but the net result is the same. As a millionaire in the making, your focus will revolve around becoming a world-class performer, which in business means *world-class problem solver*. Great problem solvers are always in demand, and that offers you maximum security. To secure yourself financially, you'll want to build and maintain substantial cash reserves and insurance instruments to cover catastrophic issues. Whether you choose to build your fortune as a high-level employee of a multinational corporation, like GE's Jack Welch or Apple's Steve Jobs, or you stake your claim as a small business owner or professional, the bottom line is the same: the better performer you are, the more security you'll have. And the more assets you acquire, the longer you can thrive through the natural and economic storms that life throws at you.

QUOTE:

"Never surrender security for opportunity"—Branch Rickey

ACTION STEP:

Surrender you security by speaking up more in school.

CRITICAL THINKING QUESTION:

Why are people addicted to security?

MILLIONAIRE RESOURCE:

Read: Brainstorm: The Power and Purpose of the Teenage Brain, by Daniel J. Siegel, M.D.

CHAPTER 57

Build a World-Class Team

There's an old saying among the self-made super rich: "it takes a team to build a dream." With few exceptions, world-class success requires the efforts of a team of dedicated professionals who are obsessed with the same vision. Even professions like law, medicine, accounting, singing, dancing, and acting; that appear to be individual, are still supported by a team of talent. In addition to developing your skills in your field of choice, and selling them to a specialized market, you're going to need to recruit, manage and retain a team to bring your vision into reality. The bigger your dream, the bigger and better team you must assemble. If you're thinking to yourself that building a team is like building an additional business, you're correct. World-class businesses effectively have two types of customers: *internal and external.* Your internal customer is your team. We call them customers because working for you is a choice you've made together, and like any customer, if they're not happy, they will leave. This is why some industries suffer from turnover rates of 40%+ per year. There are two major philosophies around managing and maintaining employees: The first is the old school approach of command and control, which was adopted from the military. This philosophy dictates that employees should do as they're told when they're told, and if they don't like it, they can leave. Managers who follow this strategy say; "I'm the boss, so it's my way or the highway." This is how the majority of companies have managed their teams in the past, and many still believe this is the most effective and prudent management style. The second philosophy comes from the new school of thought, which says that if you treat your employees like customers, they will be more engaged, happier and will rarely if ever, leave. This means turning employees into team members and stakeholders while creating a positive, proactive work culture. Obviously, this is a superior philosophy to command and control. Who wouldn't want to work in an environment of mutual respect and cooperation? But like everything, there's a downside to this strategy, which is that sometimes employees confuse kindness with weakness, and they push the boundaries too far. Even with this ongoing challenge, consider building and managing your team with this 21st-century approach. It might just make the difference between being moderately and ultra successful.

QUOTE:

"Teamwork does the dream work."

ACTION STEP:

Join a team and contribute as much as you can.

CRITICAL THINKING QUESTION:

What kind of team will you need to assemble to make your dreams come true?

MILLIONAIRE RESOURCE:

Read: Team Building with Teens: Activities for Leadership, Decision Making, and Group Success, by Mariam G. MacGregor, M.S.

CHAPTER 58

Embrace The Suck

Building a financial empire may be the most difficult thing you ever do— or it may come easier than you think. Multiple variables are involved in this equation, including talent, education, drive, and discipline. It may take you twenty years to earn your fortune, or you might do it in five. There's no way to know in advance, so the best thing you can do is mentally prepare yourself for the long haul. In other words, hope for the best and prepare for the worst. Vince Lombardi, a famous football coach from the 1960's, said it best: "everyone wants to win, but few people are willing to *prepare* to win." You are not most people. You are destined for greatness, and you must be prepared for any and all obstacles. I'm talking about all different types of obstacles, including those that are physical, mental and emotional. You will face all three on your path to prosperity, and you must defeat them. The US Navy SEALs, arguably the most skilled military unit in the world, call this "Embracing the Suck." They explain that when they're on a mission and the pain is severe, they encourage one another not to run away or deny the pain but to *embrace* it. I know it sounds strange, but they say when you embrace the pain and look it straight in the face, it dissipates. They say; "don't run from the suck, embrace the suck and tell it that you're not afraid. Is it any wonder that no one wants to go up against the SEALs? You'll have to be just as tough. Not physically, but mentally and emotionally. People are going to criticize you for being bold and ambitious, and for proclaiming your desire to be rich. You'll need to turn this criticism into emotional fuel that propels you. You'll suffer set backs in a business like everyone does, and you'll need to reframe these failures. When you begin to doubt yourself in the middle of the night, you must be mentally tough enough to recognize that every self-made millionaire has done the same. Embracing the suck, from a mental and emotional standpoint, is about learning to control and manipulate your emotions, especially under pressure. It's the foundation of what it means to be mentally tough.

QUOTE:

"Accept failure. Enjoy it, even. Embrace the suck. For the suck is part of the process." — A.J. Jacobs

ACTION STEP:

Revisit your last failure and embrace it as part of your education.

CRITICAL THINKING QUESTION:

Does embracing failure serve your long-term best interests?

MILLIONAIRE RESOURCE:

Read: NAVY SEAL Self-Discipline: How to Become The Toughest Warrior, by Jason Lopez

CHAPTER 59

Learn to Handle the Truth

As I've mentioned before, the most common psychological trap of the masses is self-delusion. It feels great to tell myself how great of a salesperson I am even though my numbers are terrible. It's comforting for me to say I'm husky instead of fat. It's a relief to know that I'm not rich because it takes money to make money. Emotional creatures delude themselves every day, but *you* must avoid it. You have to be tough enough to handle the realities of money, business, and life if you're going to become one of the great ones. In business, numbers and results rarely lie. Lousy numbers don't make you a lousy business person, and they have no power except that which you give them. Your numbers are simply giving you objective, non-emotional feedback. When the numbers are good, you don't have a problem. Managing the upside is easy. When the numbers are bad or disappointing, that's when you have to study them objectively, without emotion, and ask yourself what it will take to turn them around. This is no different than evaluating your grades in school. If you're getting straight A's, you have nothing to evaluate. If you're getting C's and D's, it's time to face the truth of what's happening. This isn't fun, and no matter how many years you do it, you won't ever enjoy it. That being said, success runs in cycles, and when you're in the up cycle, I promise you that the down cycle is not far away. The same goes for the opposite. Sometimes you'll experience one problem after another, and it seems as though the clouds will never clear. But rest assured, they will, and you will live to fight another day. The secret to learning to handle the truth and avoid delusion is practice and discipline. After a while, you'll learn to take a deep breath, accept the truth, and calmly and methodically move forward and fix it. When you can do this without emotional interference, you will become one of the most competent problem solvers in your field, and your success will be assured.

QUOTE:

"Denying the truth doesn't change the facts."

ACTION STEP:

Write down three reasons that people like you, and three reasons why others dislike you.

CRITICAL THINKING QUESTION:

Do you deserve the grades you're getting in school?

MILLIONAIRE RESOURCE:

Read: Mindset: The Psychology of Success, by Carol S. Dweck, Ph.D.

CHAPTER 60

Pay the Price of Success or Regret

The decisions you make and the corresponding consequences all come with a price. A decision to pursue a specific goal comes with the cost of not pursuing another. When little kids tell their parents that they want to be a fireman, a football player, and fisherman, parents know this isn't possible. Young children naively believe they can do everything at once. That's part of the fun of being a child. But you are moving into adulthood, and that means abandoning magical fantasies. As it relates to getting rich, you're going to need to focus on becoming one of the best in your field of expertise, and for that, you will have to pay the price. Let's say you love music and think you have what it takes to become a concert pianist, but you also have your sights set on a career in electrical engineering. If you're going to pursue both of these disciplines as hobbies, you might be able to become somewhat competent. But remember, *being somewhat competent won't make you rich.* Being a world-class pianist or engineer might, but to become great at one usually means releasing the other. No matter which profession you choose, you will be sacrificing the others. There's always a price to pay for everything, and this price is referred to as opportunity cost. The time it takes to become so proficient in a profession that you can earn a fortune from it doesn't allow for much else. So you make your decision and pay the price. It's not a perfect scenario, but it's necessary to attain the level of competence to make you rich. The price you want to avoid; is that of regret. The price of regret will nag, pick and pull at you for the rest of your life, so you need to avoid it at all costs. Decide to pay the price for success, and you'll never be saddled with the price of regret.

QUOTE:

"Success is paying the price. You've got to pay the price to win, to get there, to stay there." —Vince Lombardi

ACTION STEP:

Write down a time where you had to pay the price for success.

CRITICAL THINKING QUESTION:

What price will you have to pay to become a self-made millionaire?

MILLIONAIRE RESOURCE:

Read: The Power of Habit: Why We Do What We Do In Life, and Business, by Charles Duhigg

CHAPTER 61

Reject Status Symbols

Human beings have a weakness known as the need to feel important. Wanting to feel important is fine, but *needing* to feel important is a liability. Some people have a stronger need than others, but almost everyone hungers for affirmation. The truth is that no matter how successful someone is, no one has ever overdosed on affirmation. Needing to feel important leads people to acquire status symbols to ensure they are recognized as a person of significance. These status symbols can include massive homes, expensive cars, lavish jewelry and other pricey items designed to attract attention. These material goods are not a problem in and of themselves unless you can't afford them. And this status symbol issue is not the exclusive domain of the rich. The largest group of violators is the middle class or the average person. No, they're not buying Bentley's or Beach Houses, but they're spending more than they earn and going deeper into debt. They're buying things they don't even want, to impress people they don't even know. This is a formula for financial disaster. As a millionaire in the making, never rely on status symbols to make you feel important. No home you ever own or car you'll ever drive will be enough to satisfy your ego if you're starving for significance. The beautiful truth is that you are just as significant than anyone else. Use your mental toughness to turn your need for importance into a preference. In other words, you prefer that people make you feel important, but you don't *need* it. This comes with time and practice. Reject the status symbols of the masses, unless you can easily afford them.

QUOTE:

"Status symbols are medals you buy for yourself "—Bernhard Wicki

ACTION STEP:

Identify your favorite status symbol.

CRITICAL THINKING QUESTION:

Are you more motivated by status symbols or money?

MILLIONAIRE RESOURCE:

Read: Drive: The Surprising Truth That Motivates Us, by Daniel Pink

CHAPTER 62

Develop Yourself

All people, at all times, are operating their lives from their current level of conscious awareness. In other words, there are thousands of levels in which people may become aware of over the course of their lives, and the higher the level, the more evolved their views of life, and the world becomes. Remember what life looked like to you at age 5, 6 or 7? How different does it look now? The reason is that your level of consciousness has been raised dramatically over the years, and this process will continue throughout your life. While the masses evolve slowly and unconsciously, the great achievers are conscious of how they grow so quickly. They proactively seek new experiences, education, travel, study and a host of other strategies designed to catapult their consciousness. Self-development is one of the greatest secrets of the ultra successful. While the masses are focused on *entertaining* themselves, great performers are focused on *educating* themselves. They attend personal growth seminars and workshops, listen to audio recordings by successful people in their cars and watch videos of brilliant people delivering informative presentations all over the world. Within a few years, these ambitious people begin to pull ahead of their entertainment bombarded friends, and their results serve as a showcase of their education. As part of your grooming for greatness, we're starting your success education now, during your formative years, so you will be far ahead of the pack by the time you turn 21. The more time and energy you invest in self-development, the farther ahead you will be. Your development will not only help you become a self-made millionaire, but it will also help you be happy on the road you must travel to get there. Money won't make you happy, but it will make your life much easier and give you more choices. Learning to live in a constant state of personal growth will contribute to your happiness as well as your success.

QUOTE:

"Absorb what is useful, discard what is not, add what is uniquely your own." —Bruce Lee

ACTION STEP:

Attend a seminar on public speaking to increase your confidence and build your communication skills.

CRITICAL THINKING QUESTION:

How much personal development is enough?

MILLIONAIRE RESOURCE:

Attend the Bill Gove Speech Workshop. www.SpeechWorkshop.com

CHAPTER 63

Never Get Emotional About Money

Money is a medium of exchange: nothing more, nothing less. The world loves to make money out to be some sort of God, but it's not. It's only a means of facilitating trade. This is the objective reality of money, and when you approach it this way, it's easy to keep your emotions under control. The masses believe having money changes who you are based on what you can buy, but it's not true. The fact is that the utility value of money is convex, which means it's valuable to have a certain amount of it, but beyond that, its importance diminishes. There's no evidence to suggest billionaires are happier than millionaires. After all, how many cars can you drive? How many homes can you live in? How juicy of a steak can you eat? All of these things are nice to have, yet additional amounts serve little purpose. Is having two Ferrari's better than one? For most of us, the answer is no. If you view money through this lens, it will become infinitely easier to approach it through logic-based, critical thinking. An example of logic versus emotion-based thinking is the money people spend on new cars. Approximately 17 million Americans purchase new cars every year, yet most people know that buying a new car is one of the worst investments. It's public knowledge that you lose about 20% of the new cars value as soon as you drive it off the lot. That means if you pay $30,000 for a new car, you lose $6,000 of your investment on the first day. No investor in their right mind would be willingly to do that, unless, she was approaching the investment emotionally. How does this happen? Easily. Driving around in a brand new car makes people feel good. It makes them feel important and successful. Having the latest model is a status symbol for the masses. This is a money trap you want to avoid. Rich people rarely buy new cars for this reason. They usually purchase automobiles that are 2-5 years old, which lessens the impact of immediate depreciation. According to the research of the late Dr. Thomas Stanley, the average millionaire drives a used Ford F-150 pick up truck. That shows you how much they care about status symbols. This doesn't mean you can't drive your dream car when you get rich. You can, and if it's important to you, you should. The key is to avoid making the decision and the deal from an emotional state of mind. When it comes to growing and guarding your money, always employ your emotionless critical thinking skills, and you'll rarely suffer the regrets of irrational decision-making.

QUOTE:

"If you cannot control your emotions, you cannot control your money."
—Warren Buffet

ACTION STEP:

Using emotionless critical thinking, write down what make, model and year of car you want to purchase in the future and ask your parents to evaluate your decision.

CRITICAL THINKING QUESTION:

Do you spend your money logically or emotionally?

MILLIONAIRE RESOURCE:

Read: Buy-ology: Truth and Lies About Why We Buy, by Martin Lindstrom and Paco Underhill

CHAPTER 64

Use Leverage

If hard work were the way the wealth, every cocktail waitress and construction worker would be rich. They're not, and most never will be. Wealth is built through leverage and in many different ways. The rich are masters at leveraging their contacts, credibility, money, education, other people's money, and just about anything else you can think of to create large results with little effort. For example, while you might think that the people with the least amount of money are the biggest borrowers, it's not true. The biggest borrowers are the rich, the very people who don't need loans. They don't take them because they need them; they take them as a method of leveraging lenders money while their money sits safely on the sidelines. Savvy business owners ask banks for credit lines to use their money for investments the business could technically afford to make, but strategically would be too risky. As these lines of credit are utilized and paid back with interest, the bank increases the line of credit. As trust and repayment history are established, these lines of credit can become large enough for the business to make investments to help it grow faster. Another use of leverage is through other people's credibility. Years ago I served on a national committee chaired by President George W. Bush. The other members of the committee were all rich movie stars and political insiders. Needless to say, whenever I need something in Washington or Hollywood, the first thing I do is place calls to these people. That's simply using the power of their credibility to help me get what I'm after. Now, granted, I could do it the hard way. This is what the masses do, and while it's honorable, it's not very effective. For better or worse, the rich and powerful run the world, and you're either on the inside or the outside. You're going to hear people say this is wrong, and maybe even claim that it's corrupt. And they may be right. But the bottom line is that's how it is, and that's how it will always be. Instead of complaining about it, just get on the inside.

Another effective use of leverage is the education and information. The more you know about your field of choice, the more people will seek you out for help and the richer you will become. While your friends are playing and partying, you should be studying your field of choice to lengthen your lever. Hard workers toil and sweat for every penny they earn, while the rich leverage their hard work to earn fortunes without breaking a sweat. Sound unfair? It's not because, in a free market, everyone has the choice to use leverage instead of hard work, yet most are too lazy and fearful to take the risk.

QUOTE:

"You never get what you deserve; only what you have the leverage to negotiate." —Jalen Rose

ACTION STEP:

Make friends and build relationships with the smartest and toughest kids in your class. Leverage the smart kids to help you get better grades and the tough kids to protect you from bullies.

CRITICAL THINKING QUESTION:

Would you rather climb the ladder of success on your own or with the help and support of others?

MILLIONAIRE RESOURCE:

Read: Never Eat Alone, by Keith Farrazzi

CHAPTER 65

Getting Rich is Simple

Getting rich in America is not easy, but it *is* simple. Find a problem a solve it. The bigger problem you solve, the richer you will get. And in a free market economy, that's all there is to it. It's a simple process that anyone can follow. Complex problems require complex, innovative solutions that are both practical and cost effective. And there are lots of smart people searching for solutions, so the competition is fierce. The secret is specializing in solutions to problems in a field in which you have extensive experience and knowledge. Mark Zuckerberg may not have been a world-class baseball player, but he built a billion-dollar empire connecting college kids through Facebook. Bill Gates may not have made any money writing the great American novel, but he became the richest man in the world as the founder of Microsoft. Oprah Winfrey might not have become a great auto mechanic, but she became the first black female billionaire with her world famous talk show. Could these people have earned fortunes in other fields? Possibly, but the odds are against it. Part of the simplicity of getting rich is acquiring money in a field in which you possess more information, talent, and experience than your competitors. This gives you a major strategic advantage as it relates to seeing the problems of a specific field with uncommon clarity. It also reduces your competition, because the only people who can compete with you are those with similar expertise and experience. This is how you stack the deck and increase your odds of winning. Stay away from investing in areas that you don't know well because the experts will be almost impossible to beat. Most people know a little about a lot of fields. Your goal is to know a lot about a little. The old saying is that to become a true expert, you have to be an "inch wide and a mile deep." This is a solid strategy, as long as someone will pay to access your extreme knowledge.

QUOTE:

"If I had 60 minutes to solve a problem, I'd spend 55 minutes defining it and 5 minutes solving it." —Albert Einstein

ACTION STEP:

List three reasons that you want to be rich

CRITICAL THINKING QUESTION:

Are you practicing your problem-solving skills in school so you will be proficient by the time you graduate?

MILLIONAIRE RESOURCE:

Read: The Highly Paid Expert, by Debbie Allen

CHAPTER 66

The World Wants To Make You Rich

The world is loaded with problems, which is your opportunity to solve one of them and get rich. The masses tend to believe that the world is conspiring to keep them poor, but the truth is the exact opposite. Solving problems for society raises the standard of living for all of us. We celebrate our inventors, innovators and problem solvers, especially in America. We make heroes out of people like Steve Jobs, Elon Musk, and Bill Gates, and we have gladly made them rich in exchange for adding value to our lives. As the world grows in complexity, it will require more creative and complex solutions. The good news is we are eager to employ these new solutions, integrate them into our lives, and make the creators rich. This is something to keep in mind as a future millionaire. You'll hear adults of influence claim that the rich are trying to keep the poor and middle class down, but it's not true. The wealthier the majority of the population becomes, the more money they have to spend and invest in the products and services that the rich create. As the masses become more successful, all of the social benefits. And that's why the world wants to make you rich. Because it means you've made a massive contribution to societies standard of living. Now, this doesn't mean that your friends, family, and acquaintances want you to be rich. There's a lot of jealousy generated when someone breaks out of his or her families economic class. But the world as a whole will gladly make you as rich as long as you are solving their problems.

QUOTE:

"A wise person should have money in their head, but not in their heart"
—Jonathan Swift

ACTION STEP:

Start reading biographies of self-made millionaires.

CRITICAL THINKING QUESTION:

If someone creates a product or service that makes your life better, are you willing to help him or her become rich by purchasing it?

MILLIONAIRE RESOURCE:

Read: Elon Musk's Best Lessons for Life, Business, Success, and Entrepreneurship, by Andrew Knight

CHAPTER 67

Separate Truth from Fact

One of the most important lessons in life is learning to make distinctions in thinking. This is critical to your success because what you think determines what you believe, and what you believe will determine your behavior. One of these distinctions is the difference between truth and fact. In Mental Toughness Training, we define a fact as something that is objective, indisputable and unchangeable. We define truth as something that is subjective, disputable and changeable. In other words, the truth is a perception held by an individual that may or may not be a fact. It's critical to know the difference, especially as it relates to money and success. For example, the masses will tell you that making money is difficult. Is that truth, or a fact? It's truth, a perception because many wealthy people will tell you that making money is simple—and they're the people who have actually done it! Why do the masses say it's difficult? Mostly because that's what they've been brainwashed to believe by people who don't understand how to earn money. As with many beliefs held by the masses, they are false, yet passed down from generation to generation. This is one of the reasons most people struggle with money their entire lives. Their chance to be financially successful is over before it even begins. That's why it's critical for you to understand that most of the limiting beliefs the masses state as being fact are really only their self-defeating perceptions. The facts about getting rich in any first world country with a free market are clear and simple. All that's required is the solution to a problem that people are willing to pay for.

QUOTE:

"We can complain because rose bushes have thorns, or rejoice because thorn bushes have roses"—Abraham Lincoln

ACTION STEP:

List 3 things in life that you thought were facts, but were actually truths.

CRITICAL THINKING QUESTION:

What is the danger of following a truth that you thought was a fact?

MILLIONAIRE RESOURCE:

Read: Perception vs. Reality in Youth Sports: Understanding The Real World of Kids and Sports Through The Experiences of Successful Athletes, by J.A. Patterson

CHAPTER 68

The Masses Are Terrified

The common mindset of the masses is fear and scarcity. It's built into most of us from infancy and grows stronger throughout our lives. The main reason that so few people transcend this fear-based mindset is due primarily to its pervasiveness. When everyone around you is operating from fear and scarcity, it's contagious. Another reason is that it's so easy to prove. After all, rich people are the exception, not the rule. It's easy for people of influence to point to all the examples of poverty, famine, and failure. The world is full of those examples. As a matter of fact, the history of the world is dominated by war, which has been driven by fear, greed, and power. So the case for fear is easy to make, and it's cited millions of times every day around the world in our schools, churches, public squares, and just about everywhere else where adults have influence over young, impressionable minds. When it comes to making money, the fear of failure keeps people from pursuing their passions and chasing their dreams. Most people never make it past the fear-based advice they receive from friends and relatives, who talk them out of following their dreams to protect them from failure. What the masses fail to grasp, is that ultimate failure is *imminent.* In other words, none of us is going to live forever. The average life span is around 25,000 days, and then we are done. Our bodies eventually fail, and then our time is over. That's objective reality, a fact that none of us can alter. So if ultimate failure is imminent, where is the logic in fearing failure? We already know the way this game is going to end, so why fear anything that offers us a chance to make our dreams come true? Philosophers have pondered this question for thousands of years, and while the answer is obvious, the masses insist on allowing fear to shield them from the truth. The only thing that matters is that you reject the fear and lack consciousness of the crowd. Decide what you want and pursue it fearlessly. If you fail, start over and persist until you succeed. When fear tries to stop you, look it straight in the eyes and say: “I’m bigger than you, and no matter how many times I fail, I will not stop until I succeed.”

QUOTE:

“Choose growth over fear”—Larry Wilson

ACTION STEP:

Ask one of your teachers in school this question: *If people know they are going to die someday, why are they so afraid of failure?*

CRITICAL THINKING QUESTION:

Why do you think people are so deathly afraid of failure?

MILLIONAIRE RESOURCE:

Read: Play to Win, by Larry Wilson

CHAPTER 69

Never Stop Thinking

Thinking is the highest paid, hardest skill in the world. This is especially true as it relates to solving problems for which people will pay. Most attempted solutions won't work. This is why you must always be mentally engaged in strategic thinking in your area of expertise. Most people turn off their thinking when their workday ends at 5 o'clock, but this is not for you. You are going to be a millionaire, and that requires a deep commitment to never-ending thinking and problem-solving. The good news is you'll grow to love the process, especially as your ideas begin to generate money. This is another reason you need to gain specialized knowledge in an area that people care about, and for which they will pay. The more you know, the easier it is to direct your thinking towards solutions only an expert is capable of creating. The level of problem-solving required to become rich is too high for laymen and even most self-proclaimed experts. So by the time you reach this level, there is only a small group of people capable of coming up with possible solutions. This limits the competition you'll face and increases your odds of success. Even some of your brightest competitors will avoid thinking during their off hours, and this is where you have the opportunity to get ahead. While they're sleeping, surfing online or sending text messages, you should be *thinking*. If you implement this strategy, the only people you'll have to compete with will be the best of the best. And if you're operating from a love and abundance mindset, you'll see that competition at the highest level only makes you smarter and better. The great ones push each other to reach higher levels. Everyone at the top is trying to outdo his or her competition, which only ensures the upward ascent of everyone involved. Use both competitive and creative thought to rise above your challengers and achieve your dreams.

QUOTE:

"We cannot solve problems with the same thinking that created them"
—Albert Einstein

ACTION STEP:

Start thinking about, what you think about, and how these thoughts are helping or hurting you.

CRITICAL THINKING QUESTION:

Are you spending more of your time thinking about problems or solutions?

MILLIONAIRE RESOURCE:

Read: Atlas Shrugged, by Ayn Rand

CHAPTER 70

Money is Good

Throughout your life, you're going to be exposed to a lot of inaccurate beliefs about money. As a matter of fact, you're going to hear more misinformation about money, success, and rich people than any other subject. You might be wondering how the masses claim to know so much about something in which they possess so little knowledge? Good question and I wish I had the answer. The bottom line is that you're going to be bombarded by how bad money, wealth and rich people are. Don't believe it. Money is good. Being rich is even better. And rich people are among the most fascinating sentient beings you'll ever meet. They earned their money honestly, through ingenuity, thinking, and sacrifice, just as Adam Smith would have expected. If you're not familiar with him, research Adam Smith and his ideas on capitalism. You'll probably need to explain it to your teachers some day. Money is good because the abundance of it has the power to lift people out of poverty, raise the overall standard of living, and create opportunities that can't be offered any other way. Having money means the power to live life on *your own terms*. It means never being beholden to anyone, for anything. It can even make the difference between life and death if you're sick and need cash for the cure. Is it true that some people abuse the power money gives them? Yes. But that has more to do with the character of the abuser than the power of money. Good people don't abuse, bully or oppress others, no matter how much money they have. Money doesn't change people; it simply reveals their character. That means, as you get rich, you need to stay true to who you are. Always remember where you came from, and know in your heart that being rich doesn't make you any better than anyone else. Be grateful for your good fortune and money will be good to and for you.

QUOTE:

"Wealth is the product of man's capacity to think"—Ayn Rand

ACTION STEP:

List the three most important character traits of a good person.

CRITICAL THINKING QUESTION:

Will you treat people as well when you're rich as you do right now?

MILLIONAIRE RESOURCE:

Read: The Wealth of Nations, by Adam Smith

CHAPTER 71

Talk Yourself Up

Human beings are programmable, and the fastest way to train your brain for success is through persistent, positive self-talk. In other words, what you say when you talk to yourself will have a major impact on your beliefs, behaviors, and self-image. This empowering method of programming will offset many of the limited beliefs you will hear from your teachers. The masses are made up of people that operate from fear and scarcity, and this mindset is manifested in the language they use with themselves and others. Never bow to beliefs you know to be negative or disempowering, and always tell yourself positively, uplifting and encouraging things that will keep you moving forward. Refuse to be angry with people who speak negatively about you. The truth is that they are operating from their current level of conscious awareness, which in most

cases, is jam-packed with fear. Tell yourself daily that you are smart, focused and ambitious. Never be afraid to talk yourself into positive, proactive behaviors that you wish you exhibited, but in which you are currently falling short. This is not lying to yourself; it's programming your brain to make your actions congruent with your words. Tell yourself everyday that you are an excellent student that always goes the extra mile to complete your work to the best of your ability. Also, your work is always on time. Tell yourself that you are the master of extra credit, which helps boost your grade point average in the classes in which you excel and preserves it in the classes that don't come quite as easy. Include the message that you always build great relationships with your teachers to show them you are eager to learn. Teachers favor kids they like and are more forgiving if you encounter a problem. Talk yourself up in every area of life, and your actions will eventually follow.

QUOTE:

"Be careful how you are talking to yourself because you are listening"
—Lisa Hayes

ACTION STEP:

Write down 5 positive statements about yourself and repeat them every day to yourself.

CRITICAL THINKING QUESTION:

Is what you're saying to yourself helping or hurting you?

MILLIONAIRE RESOURCE:

Read: What to Say When You Talk to Yourself, by Dr. Shad Helmstetter

CHAPTER 72

Rich People Are Not Always Smarter

The masses have many false beliefs regarding the rich. This is partly due to their lack of exposure to the self-made wealthy, and partly due to the envy and jealousy they feel towards this segment of society. One of these beliefs, although they rarely admit it, is that rich people are smarter than everyone else. And while there is certainly a percentage of rich people who are extraordinarily intelligent, most of them are no brighter than the average person struggling to make ends meet. Your schoolteachers, for example, are well-educated professionals of considerable intelligence. Most of them will never be rich, but that doesn't mean they're not as smart as most of the millionaires in your hometown. Getting rich is less about intellect and more about focusing on the accumulation of wealth. This doesn't mean you shouldn't gather all of the education you can get. You should. The smarter you are, the easier life will be regarding riches and everything else. Never deny the role that education, both general and specific, plays in the construction of a successful, fulfilling, happy life. This doesn't mean people who are smarter or more educated should intimidate you. Everyone has a unique set of talents they're born with and others that they develop, and neither makes them better than anyone else. The bottom line is to know the facts about the impact being smart has on getting rich. It makes success an easier road, but it's not the most important skill. Focusing on the accumulation of money is the golden ticket. And if you can accomplish that, while doing something you love to do, you've won the ultimate prize.

QUOTE:

"Wealth is not a matter of intelligence, it's a matter of inspiration" —Jim Rohn

ACTION STEP:

Write down the three things you are most focused on?

CRITICAL THINKING QUESTION:

On a scale of 1-7, 7 being most focused, how focused are you on getting good grades in school?

MILLIONAIRE RESOURCE:

Read: How Children Succeed: Grit, Curiosity and the Hidden Power of Character, by Paul Tough

CHAPTER 73

Don't Delude Yourself

Human beings are highly susceptible to self-delusion. The alcoholic deludes himself into believing he has a disease, instead of a horrible habit. The fat woman tells herself she is big boned, instead of an emotional eater. The broke person tells himself fate has frowned upon him, instead of taking responsibility for his fiscal failure. Self-delusion can even extend beyond one's own psychology, as it did when a group of highly educated men flew airplanes into the Twin Towers, believing that killing innocent people would earn them heavenly rewards. Self-delusion even led Adolf Hitler to believe exterminating six million Jews was the right thing to do. Self-delusion can be local or global, the negative results minor or world changing. The fact is you're going to be surrounded by smart, educated, yet delusional people your entire life. People are emotional animals, and they use delusion to cope with the realities they are too weak to handle. As a future self-made millionaire, this is not for you. Because you are human, you will be tempted to delude yourself, and like everyone else, you will sometimes fall prey to this low level of thinking. It's easy to do, but if you guard against it, you will live most of your life in a mental state of objective reality. You'll see yourself, your circumstances and the world the way they really are, instead of the way you wish they were. This will give you an advantage over your competitors, especially as you become more and more successful. The trap door of self-delusion is easier to fall into when you're successful because you can afford its luxury. Always be on the lookout for the delusions of elevated self-importance, ego, and personal grandiosity. When you're rich, people will tell you how great you are, and if you start to believe them, it will lead to a fall. Good, bad, exciting or terrifying, always live in objective reality, and you'll be far ahead of nearly everyone in the world.

QUOTE:

"Nothing is so difficult as not deceiving yourself"—Ludwig Wittgenstein

ACTION STEP:

Write down three things that you have deluded yourself about in the past.

CRITICAL THINKING QUESTION:

How often do you delude yourself, and what does it cost you?

MILLIONAIRE RESOURCE:

Read: Extraordinary Popular Delusions and The Madness of Crowds, by Charles Mackay

CHAPTER 74

You Can Have It All

The masses suffer from either/or syndrome: they believe if you succeed in one area of life that you have to settle for less in the others. And while success certainly requires sacrifice, it's usually possible to *have it all*. I define "all" as success, fulfillment, and happiness. These are the big three everyone wants, whether they know it or not. Success without fulfillment is hollow. Fulfillment without success is struggle. And success and fulfillment without happiness are worthless. Having it all means accomplishing these three things, and make no mistake: not only is it possible, but millions of people are living it every day. Now to be clear, it's millions out of 7 billion people on the planet, half of which barely have access to food and clean water. But the proof is in the numbers of people who seem to have it all. The question is if they can do it, why can't you? The answer is you can, but remember that you're going to be told the opposite by almost everyone. The truth is that very few people have ever even attempted it. The secret to having it all begins with knowing what you want in the first place, and while this seems easy, only a small percentage of people ever figure it out. Solving this mystery comes through sustained thought and introspection, which begins with asking yourself a series of emotional questions. The most important question is what makes you feel fulfilled and happy. Activities that give you a sense of purpose and emotional fulfillment are the highway on which happiness is paved. Once you determine the activities that make you happy, your next step is to find a way to make a living doing it or something related. This is the hidden treasure of the rich. The masses think the rich are workaholics, but the truth is they would often do the work they're doing for free because they enjoy it so much. When it comes to forging the foundation of your fortune, this will be your initial task.

QUOTE:

"When you're doing something you love, the only reward you need is the experience of doing it."—Bill Gove

ACTION STEP:

Write down 5 things you'd like to have in your life.

CRITICAL THINKING QUESTION:

What's most important to you: success, fulfillment or happiness?

MILLIONAIRE RESOURCE:

Read: How to Have It All, by Christina Guidotti

CHAPTER 75

Do or Die

Most people who dare to stake their claim are shocked to discover that success is more difficult than they originally imagined. Their dreams of great wealth, recognition, and status are usually dashed during their first attempt at glory, and most of them never recover. Am I suggesting they disappear from the face of the earth? No. But for all intents and purposes, they disappear from the band of strivers and quietly slip back into the mediocrity of the masses. The pain and public embarrassment of their initial failure are too much to bear, so they bury their dreams and slink back to living a normal life, where they can comfortably and anonymously live without risk. As a future millionaire, this is not the life for you. Once you decide on the career or business that will serve as the foundation of your fortune, you must become comfortable with being uncomfortable. In other words, you have to be able to thrive in an environment of uncertainty for extended periods of time. The odds are that your first attempts will fail, but remember that most millionaires build their fortunes on what they learn from past failures. You must approach your work with a do or die mentality that refuses to surrender. Financial success is a zero-sum game, in that you either win or lose. In other words, you either have more money than you need, or you don't. There is no in between. The masses reject this idea, which is one of the many reasons they lose at the money game. Like all great goals, getting rich will require your full attention and commitment. It's not a hobby or a toy to be played with; it's more of a war that must be won.

QUOTE:

"Never say die"—Black Sabbath

ACTION STEP:

List one area of your life where you have a never say die attitude.

CRITICAL THINKING QUESTION:

If you had a never say die attitude in more areas of your life, would you be more successful?

MILLIONAIRE RESOURCE:

Read: The Art of Persistence, by Michael Stawicki

CHAPTER 76

Associate with Winners

The world consists of two groups, the winners, and the wannabes. The winners get what they want out of life, and the wannabes sit around wondering how they did it. Statistics show that the winners aren't any smarter than the wannabes, but they are certainly more driven and mentally tough. Deep down the wannabes long to have the life of the winners, but they stop short of taking action because of the fear-based mentality that guides them. This is a fact of life the masses don't like to talk about, and I don't blame them. I mean, who would want to go through life knowing they had what it took to succeed but lacked the guts to go for it? So instead of staring objective reality straight in the eyes, they delude themselves by making excuses. This is why it's crucial that you associate with winners that are actively pursuing their goals and dreams. It doesn't mean they have to be successful, it just means they have to be pursuing success the way all champions do: with determination, courage and a world-class work ethic. These associations should start in school at the youngest possible age, where you're befriending the kids who get the best grades and have the best attitudes. Stop hanging out with the "cool kids" and start spending time with the winners. You'll discover later in life that the "cool kids" usually don't go very far. High school heroes often become real-world zeros. Being cool is overrated. Being successful is better. Success in school sets the stage for success at work, and that's why you need to learn from the kids who are succeeding, whether they are popular or not. As you get older, you'll discover how the winners influenced you and became a critical component of your success.

QUOTE:

"You become who you associate with. Look around at your five closest friends, and that's who you are. If you don't want to be that person, you know what you gotta do." —Will Smith

ACTION STEP:

Write down the 5 people with whom you spend the most time.

CRITICAL THINKING QUESTION:

Are your five closest friends helping or hurting you?

MILLIONAIRE RESOURCE:

Read: Networking with the Affluent, by Dr. Thomas J. Stanley

CHAPTER 77

You Can Be Spiritual and Rich

Many people believe that all rich people care about is success and money. This is not true. Yes, the rich get rich for a reason, and that's because they focus on becoming financially independent. While the masses are spending their free time memorizing box scores and playing fantasy football, the rich are investing their time building the life of their dreams. Successful people are no less spiritual than the masses, although they often reject societal dogma and religious indoctrination. Champions tend to think for themselves and base their beliefs on evidence, rational thought, and critical analysis. Some of them are traditionally religious while others identify themselves as more spiritual. The bottom line is the rich have just as healthy of a spiritual life as the middle class or any other sector of society. Being spiritual ranges from religious to secular beliefs, but the net effect of their mindset, whatever its origin, is peace of mind and emotional tranquility. Ignore people who tell you that the rich are heartless, money-making machines. After interviewing over 1,200 of the wealthiest people in the world over 34 years, I can assure you that the masses are wrong about them. You can be as spiritual as you wish while making more money than you'll ever need. And when once you're a millionaire, you'll be inundated with religious organizations begging you for money. They may not think much of rich people, but when they need money, it's the first group they call. Prepare to be demonized by some of these organizations for your ambition to become successful. It's part of the price you pay for building a life of uncommon success in a world that worships mediocrity.

QUOTE:

"The goal of spirituality is to bring such happiness, which nobody can take away from you." —Ravi Shanker

ACTION STEP:

Read one religious or spiritual book every year to deepen your understanding.

CRITICAL THINKING QUESTION:

Are you more spiritual or religious?

MILLIONAIRE RESOURCE:

Read: The Spirituality of Success: Getting Rich with Integrity, by Vincent M. Roazzi

CHAPTER 78

Always Do What's Right

Along with your path to prosperity, you'll be tempted to take shortcuts, and once you're rich, you'll be able to buy your way out of problems. And while there's nothing wrong with using your resources to get ahead, always be sure that your actions and behaviors are ethical and fair to all concerned. Many things can be bought, but integrity is not one of them. Always do what you say you'll do even when your wealth grants you the power to get around it. This is especially important when dealing with people with whom you have authority. Using money and power to advance your success is fine, as long as you're not abusing it to harm others. Money and power don't change people, they simply reveal who they truly are. Never allow your ego to guide your actions, for the ego is an insatiable, emotionally fueled monster. Instead, operate from your spirit-based consciousness, which is always grateful and satisfied, and only wants the best for everyone. People will offer you endless praise for your financial success but never buy into the idea that it makes you smarter or better than anyone else. Smell the wonderful aroma of the praise perfume, but never *drink it.* Be nice to people and help them when you can, even when there's no personal benefit. If you're so inclined, donate time and money to causes you care about. It will give you a sense of fulfillment. You'll be judged by the way you treat the people who can't help or hurt you, and while you'll forget these interactions immediately, they may remember your kindness for a lifetime. Wield your power with caution, care, and humility. Be thoughtful and patient. Not because it will make you richer, but because it's the right thing to do.

QUOTE:

"Doing the right thing has power"—Laura Linney

ACTION STEP:

Write down one difficult or challenging situation you are currently experiencing and the right way to handle it.

CRITICAL THINKING QUESTION:

Is it always right to do the right thing?

MILLIONAIRE RESOURCE:

Read: Making Good Choices: Guide for Teens, by Purvis Atkinson

CHAPTER 79

Reframe Past Experiences

The way you feel about yourself, the world and life in general will largely be dictated by the way you frame past experiences. The good experiences you remember will make you feel happy and grateful, but the bad experiences have the power to diminish or destroy those feelings. We have all had bad experiences in life, no matter how rich or poor we may be. That's why reframing negative past experiences can have such a positive impact on the way we feel. Being bullied in school is traumatic for anyone, but reframing the bullying as a lesson in self-restraint when wielding power turns it into a lifelong philosophy. And from the moment you reframe this experience, it begins to generate feelings of well-being. Losing a loved one is an experience that often hijacks a person's happiness, but remembering all the good times creates a sense of solace and eventually begins to dissipate the depression. Reframing works on both major and minor experiences. A minor example would be feeling bored in school. Most kids would see this as a negative experience, but someone trained in reframing would see it as a sign that your level of intelligence exceeds the current school work or class in which you're enrolled. In this circumstance, a middle-class thinker would use his or her superior intellect as an excuse not to pay attention to the teacher. The world-class performer would attempt to assist the teacher in helping the other students understand the material, which would in return help him or her understand it even better. Positive reframing not only makes you feel better about the past, but it also helps you build a better future. The only downside is that it's easier to wallow in the self-pity of the present or past than it is to reframe them. The average person usually chooses the path of least resistance, and that's why you should take the opposite route. To build an extraordinary life, you have to be willing to do things the average person refuses to do.

QUOTE:

"A good laugh and a long sleep are the two best cures for anything"
—Irish Proverb

ACTION STEP:

Reframe a negative experience you've had to make it more positive.

CRITICAL THINKING QUESTION:

Could the simple habit of reframing change your life?

MILLIONAIRE RESOURCE:

Read: Reframing: Neuro-Linguistic Programming and the Transformation of Meaning, by Richard Bandler and John Grinder

CHAPTER 80

Feed Your Vision and Starve Your Fear

Your mental energy is a finite source of power of which you have complete control. Where you choose to direct it, and how intensely you focus it will determine 90% of your success. The masses squander their mental energy on trivial matters such as entertainment, sports, parties, alcohol, drugs, etc. The focus of their psychological power is divided among so many things that it's barely enough to live a mediocre existence. And by the end of the day, fatigue sets in and there's only enough energy to finish mundane tasks and sleep. This is a formula for losing. Instead, decide on the one major goal that will help you most during the day, and then focus the majority of your mental energy towards it. Champions refuse to waste their precious mental energy on fear-based thinking or worry. The great ones are famous for being laser-focused on their ultimate vision and the day-to-day steps necessary to make it a reality. There's an old saying that supports this strategy: "Feed your vision and starve your fear." The more you focus your thinking on something, the more it grows and the stronger it gets. Winners develop a healthy obsession with their goals and dreams, and this is one of the secrets of their success. Does this mean you should avoid thinking about fun, entertainment, and relaxing activities outside of your vision? No. As a matter of fact, you should devote a small part of each day to mindless relaxation and fun. This will help you lead a more balanced life and prevent you from burning out. I call this the 90/10 Formula. 90 percent of your waking hours should be invested in the active pursuit of your dreams, and the remaining 10% should be spent on hobbies, sports, or any other form of healthy entertainment. If you're awake 16 hours per day, then you have 1.6 hours every day to goof off. The remaining the 14.4 hours of laser focus will make you a champion.

QUOTE:

"Create the highest, grandest vision possible for your life, because you become what you believe." —Oprah Winfrey

ACTION STEP:

Just for today, direct 100% of your mental energy towards your vision.

CRITICAL THINKING QUESTION:

On an average day, what percentage of your focus is directed towards your vision, and what percentage is directed towards your fear?

MILLIONAIRE RESOURCE:

Read: Vision Box Idea Book: Mixed Media Projects For Crafting the Life of Your Dreams, by Mark Montano

CHAPTER 81

Learn to Listen

The most successful people in society are usually the best listeners. This is due primarily to the fact that success and solid relationships go together, and strong listening skills forge healthy relationships. In a world overrun by communication technology, active listening skills are becoming rare. Over 50% of the people who visit professional therapists cite their reason as simply having someone to listen. As you're going through school, you won't hear much debate about the importance of listening. Everyone seems to agree. The problem is only a tiny percentage of people are actually practicing it. This is because active listening requires discipline, patience, and understanding. While most people are listening to others, they are thinking of what they're going to say next. World-class listeners don't do this. They stay in the moment and attempt to feel the emotion being expressed beyond the words. They listen to others as if they were the most important people in the world, and this is obvious to the person speaking. It takes discipline not to jump in when you're listening to someone talk. And it takes patience to listen when someone is speaking at length about something you're not interested in. But perhaps the most difficult piece of the active listening puzzle lies in the effort to understand what's being said, both explicitly and implicitly. When people feel understood, an emotional bond is created, and it launches the relationship to a higher level. The more healthy relationships you build, the more successful you will be. Being a great listener might be the single most important skill you can possess. Practice listening to friends, family, classmates, teachers, coaches, clergy and anyone else you encounter, and in a short period of time, you will have built another million-dollar habit.

QUOTE:

"Most of the successful people I've known are the ones who do more listening than talking." —Bernard Baruch

ACTION STEP:

Interview your parents for an hour about their lives by simply asking questions and listening.

CRITICAL THINKING QUESTION:

In your daily interactions with people, do you spend more time talking or listening?

MILLIONAIRE RESOURCE:

Read: Just Listen: Discover the Secret to Getting Through to Absolutely Anyone, by Mark Goulston, M.D.

CHAPTER 82

Master Time Management

One of your goals as a future self-made millionaire should be to become a master of managing your time. The masses waste much of their time on activities with little benefit, mostly involving entertainment and pleasure. Their focus is on taking the path of least resistance, and most of them reach the end of their lives with little success to show. This is not due to a lack of talent, but a lack of effectively managing their time and energy towards activities that foster success. This is especially true as it relates to money. The masses love to spend and hate to save, while the rich hate to spend and love to save. It is any wonder that the rich get richer and the masses struggle? It's actually quite predictable. The way to master time management is through practice. Start now, while you're in school. Begin by always completing your most difficult homework assignments first. The best students make a habit of this. The reason has as much to do with being fresh and full of energy as it does with getting the tough work out of the way, so each subsequent assignment is easier. The average student procrastinates, and eventually carries the habit into adulthood and suffers the consequences. Always do the most important, difficult and beneficial tasks first; the second one's second; the third one's third, and so on. It's a simple strategy, but only a small percentage of the population follows it. The reason is that it's easier to do the simple jobs first, and there's even the possibility that you will run out of time and never complete the most beneficial projects. When it comes to making money, always do the most potentially profitable tasks first, and try to delegate the least profitable. This one kindergarten strategy will help make you rich.

QUOTE:

"Either you run the day, or the day runs you." —Jim Rohn

ACTION STEP:

From now on, always complete your most difficult homework assignments first.

CRITICAL THINKING QUESTION:

Does time manage you or do you manage time?

MILLIONAIRE RESOURCE:

Read: 15 Secrets Successful People Know About Time Management, by Kevin Kruse

CHAPTER 83

Live in Objective Reality

Objective reality is the way things are, regardless of perceptions, opinions or beliefs. The masses live in an emotional fantasy world filled with magical thinking, supernatural dreams and a mystical vision of how the world works. This is not because they're stupid, it's because they're scared. They are mostly scared of dying, partly of living, and always of suffering. The bottom line is that fear is fear, whatever its root cause, and it's no way to live. The great achievers force themselves to grow up emotionally and come to grips with life as it really is, instead of what they wish it were. Living in and operating your life in a state of objective reality helps you understand why people do what they do, live like they live, and buy what they buy. When it comes to building your fortune, this is extremely helpful. For example, if you're selling a product or service to the masses, the more emotional the appeal, the more they buy. Since the average person operates from fear, the easiest sale is the product/service that helps them overcome anxiety. If they're afraid of being poor, sell them on being rich. If they're afraid of getting old, sell them on feeling young. If they're afraid of dying, sell them eternal life. Fear is the strongest motivator of the masses, and your job is to avoid falling into this trap. Instead, discipline yourself to employ the opposite mindset, which is abundance. The objective reality of life is one of abundance, but you must have the courage to ignore your fears on the path to discovering it. Can you change the fear-based minds of the masses? Probably not, with a few exceptions. The rest will spend their entire lives living in fear, no matter how prosperous they become. Your job is to make sure you're not one of them, because if you live in fear, no amount of money or success will suffice. It's a miserable, self-induced existence. You begin living in abundance by taking full responsibility for your results in life. Never blame anyone else for your failures. When you look in the mirror, you'll see the person, for better or worse, who put you where you are. The next step is to avoid delusion and embrace the realities of life. And the final step is to reach the realization that in a free market, capitalistic society, you can be, have and do (almost) anything you desire. The abundance is real, and it's yours for the taking.

QUOTE:

"If your belief system is not founded in an objective reality, you should not be making decisions that affect other people." —Neil deGrasse Tyson

ACTION STEP:

Identify one area of your life where you're engaged in magical thinking and convert it to objective reality.

CRITICAL THINKING QUESTION:

Are you more of a magical or critical thinker?

MILLIONAIRE RESOURCE:

Read: The Demon Haunted World: Science as a Candle in the Dark, by Carl Sagan

CHAPTER 84

Strive to be World Class

No one is perfect, and you won't be either. Try your best to exhibit world-class behaviors. Being world-class means you are among the best in the world at a particular skill, behavior or attitude. It's a tall order, and you won't be able to achieve it in every area. The secret is to carefully and cautiously select the areas on where you will focus, and let the rest go. Adults of influence will encourage you, but you need to know that most won't believe this level of success is possible. Most people have never seen world-class success up close. Instead, it's something they see on TV and in movies. Their disbelief is not a reflection of your potential, but a lack of belief in *themselves.* The masses view the world through a small lens that has very little space for big thinking and grandiose dreams. This won't have any impact on your success unless you allow their small thinking to limit you. And don't waste time trying to convert them to world-class thinking. They will cling to their thinking and say your success was luck. A tiny percentage of well-meaning adults will encourage you to go for your dreams, but they probably won't suggest that you get rich. Most people see that as being tacky and obnoxious, which is one of the primary reasons they are broke. Here's what you won't hear, except from rich people: absolutely, positively, make getting rich one of your top goals. Become a millionaire in your 20's or 30's, and study how to save and invest your fortune so it grows with limited labor. Do not allow teachers, coaches, mentors, friends, family or anyone else talk you out of getting rich. Being rich makes life easier, and it's no small benefit to be able to do what you want, when you want, with whom you want, for as long as you want, without having to beg anyone for permission. Choose other areas in which to be world class because you love them. Choose to be rich because it's the most pragmatic strategy for success and it will give you endless options in life.

QUOTE:

"Know what you want. Clarity is power. And vague goals produce vague results." —Robin Sharma

ACTION STEP:

Interview someone who has achieved world-class success.

CRITICAL THINKING QUESTION:

Are your habits, actions, and behaviors more middle class or world class?

MILLIONAIRE RESOURCE:

Read: 177 Mental Toughness Secrets of the World Class, by Steve Siebold

CHAPTER 85

Don't Be a Jerk

You're being groomed to be rich, and in all likelihood, you will be. This means you'll have advantages in life that most people don't even know exist. You will live a life of privilege, and you will have power. Here's one of the most important pieces of advice I can offer you: don't be a jerk. It's easy to get carried away with your own success and begin to believe you are better than others. You're not. Success is a wonderful thing, but it doesn't give you the right to mistreat people because you can. There are jerks in the world that hurt people. Don't be one of them. Be nice. Keep your ego to yourself and check your self-importance at the door. Remember that there's always someone smarter, stronger, faster, richer and more ambitious. Life is not a competition. Life is about learning, growing and enjoying the ride. The years go by quickly, and there are no do-overs. You get one shot at life to succeed and do it right. You don't need to go on a spiritual quest or religious retreat to learn how to conduct yourself. All you need to do is follow the Golden Rule, which is to treat other people the way you would like them to treat you. Especially people you employ, have position power over, or others that can't help you. Remember that your success is a source of inspiration to people, but what will impact them the most is how you make them feel. Treat everyone with the same love, respect, and understanding, and you will be a positive force in the world. Remember that anyone with money and power can lord it over others, but the great ones exercise discipline, self-restraint and character to be sure that they project a positive, loving influence.

QUOTE:

"How people treat other people is a direct reflection of how they feel about themselves." —Paulo Coelho

ACTION STEP:

Practice treating people better, and build it into a habit.

CRITICAL THINKING QUESTION:

On a scale of 1-7, 7 being best, how well do your parents treat people?

MILLIONAIRE RESOURCE:

Read: How to Win Friends and Influence People, by Dale Carnegie

CHAPTER 86

Never Apologize for Being Rich

On your way to becoming a self-made millionaire, people will attempt to discourage you. They'll call you a workaholic, obsessed, greedy, overly intense and a host of other disparaging things. There will be other hurdles to your success, including financial issues, time management, personal problems, and ideas that don't work. Here's the bottom line: *getting rich is not for the faint of heart.* It's a psychological street fight, and only the toughest make it to the top. It's going to take everything you have to win. You'll have to be your best motivator and biggest fan. You'll have to believe in yourself even when no one else does. Most of all, you'll have to be mentally tough enough to persist through failure after failure, without losing your enthusiasm. If that seems like a tall order, you're absolutely right. It is, and that's why you never have to apologize when you make it. Once you're rich, you'd expect the people who doubted you to finally acknowledge your success, but the truth is most won't. Instead, they'll say you got lucky, and that you were in the right place at the right time. Don't make the mistake of seeking their approval, because you're likely to be disappointed. Instead, *seek your own approval*, because at the end of the day, you're the one who has to look yourself in the mirror. You must refuse to be addicted to the approval of others, and that only comes through desensitizing yourself to rejection and criticism. It's a painful process, yet it rarely lasts long. The key is making a decision to become a psychologically self-made man/woman. That doesn't mean you're going to succeed on your own, just that from an emotional perspective, you're able to stand-alone. Once you've forged your way through this process and have become rich, you'll never feel the need to apologize for your success.

QUOTE:

"If your success was earned through hard work and honesty, never apologize for it." —Frank Sonnenberg

ACTION STEP:

Just for today, work harder in school than you ever have before and see what happens.

CRITICAL THINKING QUESTION:

On a scale of 1-7, 7 being most addicted, how addicted are you to the approval of others?

MILLIONAIRE RESOURCE:

Read: The Disease to Please, by Harriet Braiker, Ph.D.

CHAPTER 87

Develop Sustained Concentration

The average person you will encounter in your life is looking for overnight success. If they set goals at all, which most won't, they will be short-term targets that deliver instant gratification. In essence, the average person has a short attention span and is unable to get himself to concentrate on one thing long enough to achieve it. This is the reason they think small; because big thinking requires sustained concentration and the emotional endurance to hang tough. You must discipline yourself to be the opposite. Dream bold dreams, and then back them up with laser focused, dogged persistence. Getting rich rarely happens fast, and is usually the net result of years of hard work, leverage and intelligent strategy. When you set a big goal, the first question to ask yourself is, "am I ready to do whatever it takes, for however long it takes, to succeed?" If the answer is yes, move forward. If the answer is no, kill the goal and set one that you can answer in the affirmative. You must be willing to endure the psychological/emotional suffering that accompanies any large goal. The masses will say you don't have to suffer to be successful, but remember that *success is a relative term*. The average person's definition of success is a roof over their head, clothes on their back and food in their mouth. And if you're living in an impoverished third world country, that's a good measure of success. Fortunately, you're one of the luckiest people alive, because you're living in the richest country in the history of the world, the United States of America. People reading this book outside of the U.S. are likely living in a wealthy country as well. So your definition of success should include financial freedom and at as early an age as possible. And if you're really bold, set a goal to live an "Unrestricted Existence" which means you get to live your life on your own terms minus any restrictions, except the laws of the land. That's what most of the 1,200 millionaires and billionaires I've interviewed value most about being rich: the ability to live life on their own terms. If this excites you, I challenge to make it your ultimate goal.

QUOTE:

"Concentration is the secret of strength."—Ralph Waldo Emerson

ACTION STEP:

Practice concentrating on one thing to the exclusion of everything else, and see how long you can go without losing it.

CRITICAL THINKING QUESTION:

On a scale of 1-7, 7 being longest, how long can you sustain your focus on one thing at a time?

MILLIONAIRE RESOURCE:

Read: Laser Sharp Focus, by Joanna Jast

CHAPTER 88

Embrace Metacognition

One of the secrets of the self-made rich is their ability to see themselves the way they really are, including their weaknesses and flaws. This allows them to focus on their strengths, and hire others to compensate for their weaknesses. One of the tools they use is known as *Metacognition,* or the ability to think about, what they are thinking about. This is especially useful when it comes to building their fortunes. Most people that dissect their own thinking arrive at the realization that the only time they really think about money is when they are worried about it. This is not for you. Every millionaire I've ever interviewed thinks about money, in positive terms, almost all of the time. It's no different than a great salesperson. The most successful salespeople think about closing sales, not just *making calls.* This focus leads to behaviors that create the desired result. Once you begin building the habit of thinking about what you think about, you'll see exactly why you are where you are in business, and in life. The reason is simple psychology: our thoughts lead to our habits, actions, and behaviors, which eventually create our results. For example, if someone is a hundred pounds overweight, is the root cause of the problem the food he's stuffing down his mouth? Is it his sedentary lifestyle? How about his lack of money to purchase healthy meals? No. The root cause of his problem is the way he thinks about diet, food, exercise and anything else that leads him to poor habits, actions, and behaviors. On the other end of the spectrum is the physically fit person. Is the root cause of his success the food he eats, or the types of exercises he engages in? No. Those behaviors are the result of the way he thinks about these things. The point is that if you can identify the root cause of any habit, action or behavior, all you have to do is modify the root to achieve any result you desire. Think about money, especially as it relates to how you can earn more of it, by serving others and solving problems. This will put you on the path to prosperity.

QUOTE:

"Metacognition is thinking about, what we think about, and if our thinking is helping or hurting us." —Larry Wilson

ACTION STEP:

Begin to monitor your thoughts during the day and write down your dominant thoughts.

CRITICAL THINKING QUESTION:

Do you think about the things that increase your sense of fulfillment and happiness?

MILLIONAIRE RESOURCE:

Read: (Article) Metacognition: The Gift that Keeps Giving, by Donna Wilson, Ph.D. www.Edutopia.org/blog

CHAPTER 89

Use Emotional Motivators

Emotion drives human behavior, yet many people deny this. When people claim how logical they are, don't believe it. Human beings live and die on emotion, and most significantly, they make *decisions on emotion*. Easy proof is the stock market. Most investors buy on greed and sell on fear. With so much money at stake, you would think investors would behave in a more sophisticated manner, but only a small percentage do. The rest allow their emotions to dictate their actions, often with disastrous consequences. And this phenomenon goes well beyond money. People marry on emotion; have children on emotion and select their occupation on emotion. The results prove the danger of this common behavior: more than 50% of marriages end in divorce. Many couples who have children say they love their kids but would have chosen to be child free if they had really thought about and

discussed it with their spouse. Approximately 70% of workers in America say that hate or dislike their occupation. This is why you must guard against emotion in decision-making. Our 30-years of research shows that world-class performers use logic to make decisions, and emotion to motivate themselves. This is one of the reasons the rich get richer while the masses struggle. Their secret is using what we call emotional motivators. These are emotion driven goals or dreams that excite the performer so much that he's willing to work around the clock to fulfill them. Emotional motivators run the gamut, from proving oneself to living in a mansion. These motivators tend to defy logic, and for motivational purposes, they are worth their weight in gold. The son that's starving to impress his father, or the daughter who gets straight A's to set an example for her siblings. One of the common denominators of emotional motivators is to gain a sense of importance, either through success or significance. This is why people will do almost anything for recognition. Napoleon said it best: "Men will die for ribbons." The first step to profiting from this is to be aware that it exists. The next step is to use it to your advantage, especially when it comes to motivating yourself. Decide what emotion is behind every action you take, and after a while, you'll see a pattern. Once you identify your strongest emotional motivators, use them to spur you along when things get tough and add additional firepower when everything is going your way. Don't judge yourself for being motivated by something that seems silly. Instead, use it as the psychological power tool that it is and move forward like a steaming locomotive towards your goals and dreams.

QUOTE:

"Human behavior flows from three main sources: Desire, emotion, and knowledge."—Plato

ACTION STEP:

Identify your strongest emotional motivator and how you can use it to improve your grades in school.

CRITICAL THINKING QUESTION:

How have you used emotion to motivate you in the past?

MILLIONAIRE RESOURCE:

Read: Start with Why, by Simon Sinek

CHAPTER 90

Never Take Your Eyes Off Money

The main reason most people aren't rich is they refuse to focus on earning, investing and saving money. Society has brainwashed them to believe that money is a dirty thing; a necessary evil that nice people don't discuss in mixed company. The topic of money is off limits, and that being poor or middle class is nobler than being rich. So most people avoid the subject altogether and only think about money when forced to. Never make this mistake. Money is one of the most important aspects of life, and without it, you will experience stress and struggle. The key is to *focus* on it. Once you identify what you want to do as a career, focus on earning, investing and saving money as your pursuing it. Enjoying, and maybe even loving your work should come first. Money won't create the emotional fulfillment that satisfying work offers, and it's not supposed to. If you hate your job but get rich doing it, odds are you won't be happy. Money is powerful, but it's still only a medium of exchange. It can buy you a fancy car and a magnificent mansion, but it cannot give you the deep sense of fulfillment of doing a job you love. The secret is to take as much time as you need to find what you love to do, and then focus on getting rich doing it. Fulfilling work without wealth equals stress, worry and sleepless nights. Wealth without fulfilling work equals a hollow, unsatisfying life. You need both to live the good life. The way you keep your eyes on money is to provide as much quality service as possible, to as many people as you can, for as long as you can. This strategy will help you match your talent to your earning potential. The next step is to spend your money wisely, live below your means, and study how to invest and save. As you get rich, you'll be tempted to buy into the myth that every millionaire drives a Ferrari and lives in a mansion. The truth is that some do, but only the ones who are super rich or foolish. When you join the ranks of the super rich, the top .01 percent of the population, you can buy your exotic car and lavish estate.

But beware of making the same mistake as thousands of professional athletes, musicians and many other newly minted rich, make: which is living way beyond their means believing that the gravy train will never end. It will. It always does. Good fortune can suddenly turn into misfortune. Be smart. Be frugal. And always know your financial position. If you follow this advice, you'll live life in abundance.

QUOTE:

"Do not save what is left after spending, but spend what is left after saving." —Warren Buffet

ACTION STEP:

Start saving 20% of your allowance and spend the rest

CRITICAL THINKING QUESTION:

What is more important, earning or saving money?

MILLIONAIRE RESOURCE:

Read: The Money Class: A Course in Basic Money Management for Teens and Young Adults, by Michael James Minyard

CHAPTER 91

Income Disparity Will Always Exist

The richer you become, the more aware you will become of income disparity, the large gap between the high incomes of the top 1% of the population and the other 99%. The people who believe this gap is unfair and should be regulated by government call it "income inequality." The people who think it's simply the difference between the producers and everyone else call it income disparity. The bottom line is that people do not, and have not ever, contributed equally to society. The great producers contribute more in a year than the masses do in a lifetime, and as a result, they are rewarded with wealth. Are there abuses and flaws in the free market system? Yes. Is the system rigged for the rich? No, but you wouldn't know it by listening to people who believe in wealth redistribution. These people believe you should work hard, be smart, take risks, get wealthy and then give them a share of your money. Meanwhile, while you were working 80 hours a week building your business or career, they were working from 9 to 5. It's an entitlement mentality. They think because you're so successful, that you should be forced, through excessive taxation, to share your money. And this is not just the philosophy of the masses, but also of many well-educated college professors, economists, and politicians. Many of them want guaranteed tenure so they can't be fired while you have to compete openly in a fierce and unpredictable marketplace. The bottom line, however unfortunate, is that income disparity will always exist at some level because in a free market, people are usually paid exactly what they're worth. The same is true for the big producers, which can be 100 times as much in exchange for creating 100 times the value. Never allow the small producers to make you feel guilty for being a large producer. By the time you're rich enough to have to navigate this moral dilemma, you'll have the scars to prove that you earned every penny you've been paid.

QUOTE:

"We may have democracy, or we may have wealth concentrated in the hands of the few, but we cannot have both." —Supreme Court Justice Louis Brandeis

ACTION STEP:

Think of one way the masses could gain a greater share of wealth.

CRITICAL THINKING QUESTION:

If worked extremely hard to get straight A's in school, would you be willing to combine your grades with the C students if your teacher would agree to give the entire class a B?

MILLIONAIRE RESOURCE:

Read: The Upside of Inequality: How good Intentions Undermine the Middle Class, by Edward Conard

CHAPTER 92

Choose Prosperity over Entertainment

How you choose to use your time will determine your future. The masses spend their time, while the rich *invest* it. The difference is simple, yet the effects are profound. Spend your time basking in entertainment, and you will struggle your entire life financially. Invest your time creating solutions to people's problems, and you'll never lose a minutes sleep worrying about how to pay the mortgage. Now, remember, the solutions you create for people must be saleable. In other words, someone has to be willing to pay for them. This is critical to crafting successful solutions. Your early prosperity boils down to deciding whether you'd rather enjoy the instant gratification of entertainment or the delayed gratification of success. The good news is 95% of people will choose entertainment. I say it's good because it means you only have to compete with remaining 5%. Needless to say, this 5% is not to be taken lightly, and the top 1% will be working around the clock to win. They will be searching for the same things as you are: big solutions with high profits and low risks. They will start early and stay late, and you'll have to do the same to compete with them. The secret is to narrow your search to solutions that excite you. This way, when you select one, you'll look forward to selling it, and you won't mind working long hours. Providing a solution without passion is a poor formula because even when you win, you lose. Again, wealth without fulfillment is a foolish strategy. Start your search for solutions in the areas of life, living, and business that you're passionate about, and never settle for something that doesn't excite you.

QUOTE:

'The ability to discipline yourself to delay gratification in the short term in order to enjoy greater rewards in the long term is the indispensable prerequisite for success." —Brian Tracy

ACTION STEP:

Do something today that will benefit you or someone else in the future.

CRITICAL THINKING QUESTION:

In school, do you spend more time entertaining yourself or learning for the future?

MILLIONAIRE RESOURCE:

Read: The Grit Guide for Teens, by Caren Baruch-Feldman, Ph.D.

CHAPTER 93

Use Gratitude as a Strategy

Bill Gove, the father of the professional speaking industry, was known for saying that "Gratitude is the aristocrat of all of the emotions." This is something you won't hear much about in school. The masses believe you should just be grateful for what you have and not attempt to go for anything beyond. The great achievers believe you should be grateful for any good fortune you have, while simultaneously striving to manifest your ultimate dream life. In other words, gratitude is a means to a more successful end as opposed to an end in itself. Operating your life in a state of perpetual gratitude is perhaps the single most underrated psychological performance strategy. It allows you to feel fulfilled and happy even in the midst of your most fierce and frustrating battles. Being thankful for what you have, and you put your mind into a state of abundance, where you feel as though you're capable of accomplishing anything. Fear does not exist at this level of thought, which means you are not relegated to thoughts, beliefs, and behaviors that might keep you in a "playing not to lose" mentality. Thoughts of gratitude towards others help you maintain harmonious relationships. The fastest way to move your mind into a state of gratitude is to list all the things you're grateful for when you first wake up in the morning. It's a simple, yet effective strategy for guaranteeing that you start the day off in a winning frame of mind. When you're in a state of gratitude, you will attract people to your fearless energy. While gratitude is an underrated success strategy, it's better known for being a *happiness strategy*. Thoughts of gratitude increase feelings of well being, fulfillment, and life satisfaction.

QUOTE:

"Learn to be grateful for what you already have, while you pursue all that you want." —Jim Rohn

ACTION STEP:

Write down something you are grateful for every day before school, and ask your parents to hang it up in the house where everyone can see it.

CRITICAL THINKING QUESTION:

Is there anyone in your life to which you need to express your gratitude?

MILLIONAIRE RESOURCE:

Read: Gratitude, by Oliver Sacks

CHAPTER 94

Separate Logic and Emotion

Not all thoughts are equal, and there are various types of thinking. Again, this is not something they teach in school; not even in the Ivy League. The strategy of world-class thinkers is using emotional thoughts to motivate and logical thoughts to steer. In other words, put the power of emotion to its highest and purest use, which is its ability to drive your heart and mind to accomplish big things. At the same time, never allow emotion to dictate strategy unless you're willing to lose everything for the *sake of a feeling.* An example would be a mother running into a burning building to save her child. Logic would stop the parent in her tracks, but the emotional love she feels for her child would override her sense of logic. Outside of an extreme situation like this, always employ logical thinking to guide your habits, actions, and behaviors. The key is separating logic and emotion and utilizing each one where it belongs. Many people mix logic and emotion and end up with a lifetime of poor decisions. The guy who marries the girl with the pretty face and ends up miserable because her heart wasn't so pretty. The girl who marries the guy with money so she can feel secure and ends up a prisoner in her own home. The party boy in college who buys a bar after graduation to recapture the memories of his youth and ends up drinking his profits; or the girl who dreamed of being the prom queen who looks for happiness in clothes, jewelry and plastic surgery. These are all common examples that are often repeated in 21st century America, and they are the direct result of using emotion based thinking in place of logic. The secret to avoiding this trap is simple: when it's in your best interests to feel something you want to feel, use emotion-based thinking. Examples are watching a movie, listening to music, or reading an inspirational quote. Use logic based thinking for serious decision-making, and for steering your mental energy in the right direction. The more you separate logic and emotion, and use them in their appropriate places, the more successful life you will lead.

QUOTE:

"When dealing with people, remember you are not dealing with creatures of logic, but creatures of emotion." —Dale Carnegie

ACTION STEP:

Write down something you purchased through logic instead of emotion, and the end result of that decision.

CRITICAL THINKING QUESTION:

Would you be a better student if you approached your classes and studies more logically?

MILLIONAIRE RESOURCE:

Read: Being Logical: A Guide to Good Thinking, by Dennis Q. McInerny

CHAPTER 95

Learn to Forgive

During the course of your life, you will gain the favor of many people who will help, protect and watch over you. And they will ask for nothing in return. They will lift you up and inspire you to do the same for others. They will act unselfishly with no ulterior motive. This is the rich, beautiful and heartening part of humanity. These people will make your life joyful. Then there will be people on the other side, who will hurt, deceive and cheat you. These people will steal your soul if you let them. They will attempt to amputate your spirit with their words and actions, and they are incapable of feeling remorse or even the slightest bit of empathy. Their actions actually have nothing to do with you. This is who they are. This is the way they were born and they way they will die. They are ruthless killers, figuratively speaking. Never fight a ruthless, heartless person unless you're willing to become one, and the mindset that requires is not the mindset you want to develop. While the killer instinct might lead to short term victories, the long-term result is misery and unhappiness. No matter how successful you may become with this mindset, no one trusts or wants to be around someone who operates this way. The only strategy you can employ to beat a killer is to *forgive him.* I'm not suggesting that you befriend or turn your back on him, no more than I would suggest befriending a black bear or turning your back on a rattlesnake. Forgiveness is a nonlinear strategy designed to release the weight of anger and resentment. Forgiveness is for *you, not for them.* Whether you forgive them or not, these people will continue to destroy everything in their path, which is why you want to stay as far away from them as possible. Your forgiveness doesn't mean you agree with their actions; it simply means you've released your anger. Your forgiveness doesn't require their consent or even their awareness of it. You don't have to tell the killer you forgive him. All you do is release the negative, disempowering thoughts and images you were previously playing in your head and move on. Tell yourself these people are simply doing what they've always done, except this time you were the person in their way, which is why you got run over. It wasn't personal; it's just who they are and what they do. So forgive them, release the anger and get out of their way before they hurt you again. And make no mistake: if you give them the opportunity, they will.

QUOTE:

"To forgive is to set a prisoner free and discover that the prisoner was you."
—Lewis B. Smedes

ACTION STEP:

Decide to forgive someone who has hurt you.

CRITICAL THINKING QUESTION:

How can being more forgiving help you become more successful?

MILLIONAIRE RESOURCE:

Read: Forgiveness is a Choice, by Robert D. Enright, Ph.D.

CHAPTER 96

Focus on Your Strengths and Weaknesses

Albert Einstein once said, "Everybody is a genius. But if you judge a fish by its ability to climb a tree, it will spend its whole life believing that it's stupid." Einstein was right. All of us have areas in which we excel and others in which we struggle. The best example is our school system, which rewards students who thrive at memorizing facts, dates and figures, and punishes those who don't. The creative daydreamers are often made to feel as if they are slow learners, yet often end up becoming some of the societies most successful entrepreneurs and innovators. In recent years, professional educators have attempted to alter their teaching methods to better accommodate different learning styles. The key is knowing yourself, both your strengths and weaknesses. Strengths are the areas of life that come easily to you; where you don't really have to try to do well, and weakness is the opposite, where every action you take is a struggle. Once you have identified your strengths and weaknesses, the secret is to *follow your strengths*. The masses try to fix their weaknesses and take their strengths for granted. This is a huge mistake. Invest your time leveraging your strengths to the highest degree, while simultaneously avoiding, or at least minimizing, the time you spend using them. The person with great math skills will probably be a better engineer than the person who thrives in the art shop. The person who loves to read will probably be a more successful writer than the person who excels in the biology lab. These are generalizations, and some people are talented in multiple areas while others are limited to a few. Your job is to find your strengths and maximize them. You'll be happier, more fulfilled and far more successful. And when someone tells you the secret to success is improving your weaknesses, nod your head politely and move forward with your strengths.

QUOTE:

"When we studied them, excellent performers were rarely well rounded. On the contrary, they were sharp."—Donald O. Clifton

ACTION STEP:

Identify your three greatest strengths and three greatest weaknesses.

CRITICAL THINKING QUESTION:

Does your greatest strength have the power to make you rich?

MILLIONAIRE RESOURCE:

Read: Strengths Finder 2.0, by Tom Rath

CHAPTER 97

Speak Publicly

95% of people are terrified of public speaking. In polls dating back to the early 20th century, the masses site public speaking as their #1 fear. This is one of many reasons that you must become a proficient public speaker. When you are onstage, the impact of your words on people is magnified. Public speaking gives you a heightened level of influence unlike any other form of communication. This is one of the reasons world-class business people invest so much time refining their speaking skills. The return on investment is second to none. In school, you'll have the opportunity to deliver oral presentations of various kinds, and your job is to take advantage of them. The time you spend preparing for each of these presentations will rank among of the best investments you'll ever make. The first step to getting over any fears you might have about public speaking is to stop caring about what other people think about you. This might sound like a strange strategy, but the fear of embarrassing themselves is the primary reason most people are scared to speak in front of a group. The secret to overcoming this irrational fear is realizing that people are far more concerned with themselves than anything you may or may not do, and they spend little time thinking about anyone else. This is not a criticism, it's a fact grounded in research. The second step is to evaluate what kind of person judges or makes fun of someone who makes a mistake during a presentation. Everyone who dares to step in front of a group will make mistakes, and some of these mistakes are embarrassing. Good people *encourage* others and the people who don't are not worth worrying about. Their response to any mistakes you make says more about them than it does about you. Once you reach these conclusions about people, public speaking isn't so scary.

QUOTE:

"Public Speakers must have the courage of a bullfighter, the patience of a nightclub hostess, and the concentration of a Buddhist monk" —Bill Gove

ACTION STEP:

Attend a local Toastmasters Club meeting with your parents.

CRITICAL THINKING QUESTION:

If you became a proficient public speaker, would it make you a better student?

MILLIONAIRE RESOURCE:

Read: Public Speaking for Kids, Tweens and Teens: Confidence for Life, by David Nemzoff

CHAPTER 98

Focus on Earning Money

You will get in life what you focus on, and earning money should be one of your primary targets. To the masses, this statement is considered self-centered, shallow and greedy. They will tell you to focus on helping others before helping yourself. This is the reason such of a small percentage of people ever become financially independent, even in a first world country like the United States where the opportunities to get rich are abundant and the streets are paved with gold. Focusing on helping other people, when they can barely help themselves, is one of the losing strategies of the poor and middle class. Helping people is wonderful, but help yourself first before attempting to save everyone around you. And while money isn't everything, it single handily solves more of life's problems than any other resource, which is why you must have it in abundance. Once you're rich enough not to worry about it, then you can help others do the same. Total focus on money might lead you to do anything to get it, so I don't recommend that approach. Instead, decide to match your talents and interests with a problem people will pay you to solve and go to work until you succeed. This formula offers you the fulfillment of doing work you love while profiting from solving other people's problems. The more problems you solve, the richer you will get. Just make sure that once you have this strategy in motion, that you focus your efforts on earning the maximum amount of money for the value you provide. Many people get so caught up in the work that they forget to focus on the financial piece of the puzzle, which is how small business people, athletes, artists and others go bankrupt despite earning enormous sums of money. So enjoy your work while keeping a watchful eye on the dollars and cents.

QUOTE:

"Your greatest asset is your earning ability. Your greatest resource is your time." —Brian Tracy

ACTION STEP:

Ask your parents what you would have to do to double your weekly allowance, and if you can do it, accept their offer.

CRITICAL THINKING QUESTION:

On a scale of 1-7, 7 being most focused, how focused are you on earning money?

MILLIONAIRE RESOURCE:

Read: I Can Earn It! The Make Money How to for Teens and Tweens, by Rachel and Bev Wood

CHAPTER 99

Prepare to Win

There's an old saying: everyone wants to win, but very few people are willing to *prepare to win*. It's an accurate statement, and this is what this book is all about. A large part of success is preparation. Physical, mental, emotional and spiritual preparation. Sports are a great example: the marathon runner trains for months to be able to be at his best during the 26.2-mile race. The football player spends the off- season in the weight room bulking up. The tennis player invests hours doing foot drills, practicing serves and mentally prepare herself for the next tournament. All of this takes place long before the main event, in the quiet darkness of early mornings and late nights. There are no cameras, reporters or fans. There's just the athlete and his dream, chipping away at his deficiencies and building on his strengths, little by little, day-by-day. No fanfare or flash, just hard work and faith that it will pay off. The same goes for succeeding in school. The average students do as little as they can get away with, while the top students invest the time and effort necessary to prepare themselves for greater opportunity. These are the kids the average student makes fun of. We had one in my class named Joe. He was a smart kid, but not any smarter than the rest of us. He studied hard, sat in the front of the class and participated in every class discussion. His homework was always on time or early. He stayed after school to help the teachers for extra credit. He dressed like he was going to his office everyday, yet he was only a kid. All the kids loved to razz him about being a professional student. It was done playfully, and even he laughed about it, but the truth is, it was no laughing matter. Joe wasn't playing a game, he was *preparing to win*. This went on for 12 years, and I'll be honest: Joe wasn't smartest kid in the school or the best student, but he outworked the kids who were. And in the spring of our senior year in high school, the top three students in our class announced they would be attending Purdue, the University of Illinois and the Bradley University. Joe was not in the top three, but guess who gave him a scholarship: Harvard. That's the power of preparing to win.

QUOTE:

"Winning can be defined as the science of being totally prepared." —George Allen

ACTION STEP:

Ask your favorite teacher how you can better prepare yourself for college.

CRITICAL THINKING QUESTION:

Are you doing all you can to prepare for your future?

MILLIONAIRE RESOURCE:

Read: How to Be a High School Superstar, by Cal Newport

CHAPTER 100

Creation Trumps Competition

In a free market society like the United States, the masses focus on beating their competition. This is not a bad thing, yet it's not the highest level of thinking that leads to world-class success and wealth. Creation is. In other words, creating innovative solutions to people's problems that no one has previously discovered places you in a league by yourself, where there is no competition. Of course once your creation is commercially successful, competition will come along. That's the nature of a capitalistic society, and it's a wonderful phenomenon that generates improved products and services while driving prices down. Once your product or service enters this phase, you move back into the creation phase and invent another innovative solution. That's how the creative innovator operates. It's not a mindset focused on beating someone, it's a mindset focused on creation. Becoming a creator begins with the approach you take to everything, including your school work. What could you create right now that would help make you and your classmates better students? Back in the 1800's, educators created the concept of recess as a way to release the tension students experienced during school. In more modern times, college students created the concept of study groups, where groups of students gather to discuss the key concepts before exams. Over the years there have been dozens of these creations that helped students get a better education. Start thinking of ways to do the same for yourself and others, and you're on your way to becoming a creator. The same goes for other areas of your life, such as sports or other after school activities. In the 1980's, our tennis team was searching for a way to make practice more fun, so we created music-based practice sessions. Other sports turn practice routines into games that make it more enjoyable. The secret to becoming a creator is simply getting started. The more you create, the better you get. And don't worry if most of your creations fail because that will place you in the company of creators like Thomas Edison, Albert Einstein and Elon Musk. Just start creating, have fun, and only compete with yourself.

QUOTE:

"Creativity is seeing what everyone else has seen, and thinking what no one else has thought." —Albert Einstein

ACTION STEP:

Write down a creative solution to help stop school bullies.

CRITICAL THINKING QUESTION:

On a scale of 1-7, 7 being most creative, how creative, how creative are you?

MILLIONAIRE RESOURCE:

Read: Creative Expression Activities for Teens, by Bonnie Thomas

CHAPTER 101

Develop World-Class Beliefs

The beliefs you adopt will determine 95% of your success, which is why you must select them carefully. Human beings are emotional animals that can be influenced to believe almost anything, and that's why you'll hear people espouse some of the most preposterous beliefs imaginable. Most of these beliefs have been handed down from our ancestors over the centuries, and are a reflection of their pre-enlightenment ignorance. The average 12-year old today knows more about the world than the average adult of the 16th century. Science has replaced mythology and explained the natural world. That being said, many people refuse to release their archaic beliefs due to the fear of operating in a world they don't understand. Even some of your teachers in school, who are formally educated people, will express beliefs that, to a student of the 21st century, are unbelievable. An example would be their beliefs about earning money. You'll hear them demonize rich people, rich corporations and anything related to excessive prosperity. Luckily, it won't be all of your teachers, but it will be a substantial enough percentage to make a note of. The secret is to identify and copy the beliefs of the most successful people you admire and install those beliefs into your consciousness through spaced repetition. This means is repeating these beliefs to yourself and others on a daily basis until they become a natural part of your mental makeup. This is how emotional creatures are programmed for success, and your job is to take control over the process, so you are consciously choosing each belief for a specific reason. Once these beliefs become a part of you, you'll begin to take action and create results. Create the belief that you are a self-made millionaire and repeat it to yourself everyday, even when it's not true. Remember, you're an emotional creature, and a belief doesn't need to be true to be believed, it simply has to be *programmed into your brain.* The human brain seeks congruence, which means it will find a way to make what you're saying the truth, which will lead you to take actions that will make you a self-made millionaire. Is this process that simple? Yes, but the masses don't believe it and probably never will. Instead, their beliefs are constructed arbitrarily, at random, and they end up with a mixed bag of empowering and disempowering beliefs, which leads them to take actions that manifest middle-class thinking and moderate success. This is not the path you want to take. You are being groomed for greatness, and that means building world-class beliefs, consciously, one at a time.

QUOTE:

"All money is a matter of belief." —Adam Smith

ACTION STEP:

Identify your three strongest beliefs about money.

CRITICAL THINKING QUESTION:

Are your strongest beliefs about money helping or hurting you?

MILLIONAIRE RESOURCE:

Read: The Unlimited Self: Destroy Limiting Beliefs, Uncover Inner Greatness, and Live the Good Life, by Jonathan Heston

CHAPTER 102

Rich People Think Differently

There are basically two groups of people that make up any first world, capitalistic society, such as the United States: one that believes you are responsible for your own financial success and the other that believes you are not. The masses believe the latter, and many of them also think that the rich are the oppressors of the poor. Don't buy into this weak philosophy. Millions of people, who start with nothing but a dream, become self-made millionaires every year, and the masses don't like it. The self-made man (or woman) is a mirror they peer into and see themselves, minus the results. Anyone with average intelligence and a burning desire to succeed can make it big in a free market country, but instead of embracing this truth, they often choose to demonize the people who do. See, it's easier to criticize the winners than it is to become one. It takes far less effort to say that the self-made rich are gaming the system and that they made their fortunes in some shady, ill-gotten way. And the masses almost always take the easy way out. While they're busy entertaining themselves with everything from sports, games, booze and anything else you can imagine, the champions are hard at work building their fortunes. But don't expect to hear this from your teachers, coaches, pastors or any other community leaders. This fact is only truly accepted by a minority of the population. After all, if the masses ever accepted it, and admitted that the self-made rich got there through sacrifice, courage and hard work, they would have to face themselves, their friends and their families and come clean about not being willing to pay the price for success. That's not likely to happen. Will some of your teachers and leaders give the self-made rich the credit they deserve? Yes, but it will be a small percentage. Just know that if you want to enjoy the success of the champions, you have to learn to think like one.

QUOTE:

"Poor people have big TV's. Rich people have big libraries."—Jim Rohn

ACTION STEP:

List three ways you can begin to take control of your own financial success while you're still in school.

CRITICAL THINKING QUESTION:

Do you believe that you have what it takes to become a self-made millionaire?

MILLIONAIRE RESOURCE:

Read: Think and Grow Rich, by Napoleon Hill

CHAPTER 103

Be a Comeback Artist

The old saying goes: "If at first you don't succeed, try, try again." What it should say is "When you don't succeed at first, or second or third..." The fact is that success rarely happens on the first attempt. Success is usually the result of months, and sometimes years, of failure after failure. This is the reason you must become a comeback artist, someone who fails again and again and keeps coming back until she wins. You may have to try every way *not to succeed* before you discover the one way that you will. The secret lies in your thinking; in your ability to keep your ego in check and your head held high as you move from failure to failure, and eventually, to success. This is not something you'll learn in school; it's something you decide to become before you ever attempt something big. Being a comeback artist doesn't mean you're expecting to fail, but that you're operating under the objective reality that shows most new ventures fail the first time out. If you happen to defy the odds, like Mark Zuckerberg did with Facebook, and you hit a home run the first time at bat, that's fantastic. Odds are you won't, but that doesn't make it impossible. Most likely your success will require a series of launches before you discover the formula that works, and that means you need to think of failure as a stepping-stone. This will keep you marching forward at full speed while your competition is wallowing in self-pity because they didn't become overnight millionaires. Many people quit after their first attempt at major league success, not knowing that their initial failure was statistically predictable. So they shrivel up like a turtle retreating into his shell. They feel embarrassed, humiliated and emotionally mortified that they have publicly failed on a grand scale. Most of them disappear back into the masses never to be heard from again. This is not for you. So let's get this straight: failure, like everything else, has no meaning except the one you assign to it. Failure to the comeback artist, while disappointing, means starting over from a more educated place, which increases their odds of success. If they fail again, it only means they're learning more with each launch. As you can predict, with this mindset, nothing can hold them back from eventual success. No one can stop the comeback artist, which is why you must become one.

QUOTE:

"You may have to fight a battle more than once to win it."

ACTION STEP:

Start telling yourself every day that you are a comeback artist.

CRITICAL THINKING QUESTION:

If you tell yourself that you are a comeback artist enough times, will you begin to believe it?

MILLIONAIRE RESOURCE:

Watch: Rocky, by Sylvester Stallone

CHAPTER 104

Operate with Class

People are emotional creatures that allow their feelings to govern their lives. This is not a great strategy, but it is the strategy most people employ. You will be judged in your personal and business relationships based on how you make people feel, and if this sounds irrational, you're absolutely right. As long as you're aware of this fact, you won't be surprised at people's reactions towards you, whether positive or negative. Your best bet for success is to operate with class in everything you do, even when you're tempted not to. It's easier to take the low road, but the fallout from the nastiness, pettiness and fear will not serve your long-term interests. You're going to be rich, and for that reason alone, people are either going to look up or down to you. The people that look up to you will admire your success, and how you make them feel will be magnified by their admiration. The people that look down on you are secretly jealous of your success, and they mask their envy through false disgust. You will positively influence both types by showing class. The more elegant you are in your words, actions and behaviors, the more influence you will gain. The average person doesn't expect the rich and powerful to operate with class. The only wealthy people the average American knows are the ones they see on TV and in movies. Hollywood loves to portray the rich as arrogant, rude oppressors of the poor and middle class, and that's often the only impression most people have. Always conducting yourself in a classy manner will destroy this falsehood and will show people that rich and classy are not mutually exclusive.

QUOTE:

"Class is an aura of confidence that is being sure without being cocky. Class has nothing to do with money. Class never runs scared. It is self-discipline and self-knowledge. It's the sure footedness that comes with having proved you can meet life." —Ann Landers

ACTION STEP:

Write down one class action you could take in the next week at school.

CRITICAL THINKING QUESTION:

On a scale of 1-7, 7 being most classy, how classy are you?

MILLIONAIRE RESOURCE:

Read: Business Class, by Jacqueline Whitmore

CHAPTER 105

Wealth Creates Freedom

By now you now that being rich won't make you happy. If you're not happy without money, you won't be happy with it. Happiness is an inside job that cannot be purchased. The best thing about wealth is the freedom it offers you. Freedom to live life on your own terms, in your own way, in your own time. Being rich allows you to live anywhere you want; do anything you want, and be anything you want to be. If you make a mistake, you can often buy your way out of it. Writing a check can solve 90% of the problems you will encounter in life. This will give you peace of mind and help you sleep better at night. If you want to start a business, take up a new sport, or learn a new language, all that's required is your decision to do it. When you're rich, money is never a problem, so you don't waste time worrying about it. If you want to donate to your favorite charity or cause, you can do so with pleasure. There are lots of needy people in the world that are worthy of your generosity. Many people find that giving to those in need is more fulfilling than loading up your garage with fancy cars and living in a castle. The truth is, when your rich, you can do all of these things and more. Being rich gives you the freedom to choose, and if you choose wrong, the freedom to choose again without stress or penalty. Wealth gives you the power to make your own rules, as long as they don't break any laws or hurt any people. It may not make you any happier, but it will certainly give you the freedom you deserve.

QUOTE:

"Financial freedom is when you never do anything that you don't want to do for money, and you never omit doing something that you want to do because of a lack of money." —Phil Laut

ACTION STEP:

Watch the movie, The Secret.

CRITICAL THINKING QUESTION:

What would you do with your life if you had unlimited financial resources?

MILLIONAIRE RESOURCE:

Read: The 9 Steps to Financial Freedom, by Suze Orman

CHAPTER 106

Be Decisive

Successful people are decisive. They make decisions quickly and change them slowly. They also make big decisions far faster than the average person. This behavior is rooted in their self-confidence. People who possess supreme self-confidence are decisive because they trust themselves to quickly evaluate the criteria of any decision and arrive at an emotionless, logical decision. They know that if their decision turns out to be wrong, they can make the best of it. This speed in decision-making gives them an advantage over their competitors, for while these people are wavering back and forth, they've already moved on to the next decision. Practice making quick decisions when you're in school, spending time with friends and with your family. Being decisive is a skill that improves with practice. The more you do it, the quicker you become, and the faster your confidence grows. The secret to mastering this skill lies in the successful results of your quick decisions. Once you realize that your first decision is usually the right decision, the fear you initially feel will subside and eventually disappear. There are exceptions to this, most of which involve situations where your emotions are running high and threaten to distort your sense of logic and rationality. In these cases, allow your emotions to return to normal levels and then make your decision. Making a decision in the midst of high emotion is equivalent to doing so when under the influence of alcohol. It's hard to make an accurate choice in the presence of an obstructive, destructive chemical force. If you're in the middle of a war zone, or in front of a speeding train, you may have no choice, but in most everyday situations, you will. So think clearly, use your sense of reason, and pull the trigger. If you make a mistake, know that you're smart enough to fix it.

QUOTE:

"The way to develop decisiveness is to start right where you are, with the very next question you face." —Napoleon Hill

ACTION STEP:

The next time you dine at a restaurant, decide on what you want to eat in 60 seconds or less.

CRITICAL THINKING QUESTION:

On a scale of 1-7, 7 being most decisive, how would you rate yourself?

MILLIONAIRE RESOURCE:

Read 365 Days of Positive Self-Talk, by Dr. Shad Helmsetter

CHAPTER 107

Be Curious

Curiosity is one of the little-known traits of successful people, and the reason is simple: The more curiosity you exhibit with other people, the more you can learn from them. Life goes fast, and no one lives long enough to learn it all, which is why it's critical that you accelerate the pace of your informal education by learning from others. And I'm not just referring to your teachers, parents, and family. Those are obvious choices, but you should also add a wide range of people that you interact with at school, in sports and any other activities. Express your curiosity by asking questions, actively listening, and asking additional questions as they're giving you the answers. Everyday people that seem to have nothing to teach you may turn out to be your greatest mentors, or they may say one thing that you carry with you for the rest of your life. People love to talk about their experiences and are usually starving to share what they've learned because, in a busy world, no one seems to have time to listen. This is a mistake because the education you can get from others by being curious is substantial. Whenever you're in a room full of people, the smartest ones are usually the people asking the questions and listening intently to the answers. It's not the talkers that learn; it's the listeners. The secret lies in the questions you ask and the attention that you pay to the person you're asking. Their answers will help you make distinctions in thinking, especially as they relate to success and failure. Sometimes they will be lessons to follow, and other times, they will be cautionary tales. Either way, you will learn and grow. Focus most of your questions around successful living and prosperity. Asking questions about their favorite color or football team won't help you. You want to know the conclusions they've reached in the areas of life that matter so you can use them to accelerate your own success.

QUOTE:

"The important thing is not to stop questioning. Curiosity has its own reason for existing." —Albert Einstein

ACTION STEP:

Write down a list of 50 questions to ask your parents about life, living and what they've learned along the way, and then ask them.

CRITICAL THINKING QUESTION:

If you were more curious about your studies in school, would you be a better student?

MILLIONAIRE RESOURCE:

Read: The Curious Mind: The Secret of Secret to a Bigger Life, by Brian Grazer and Charles Fishman

CHAPTER 108

Compartmentalize Your Emotions

Your ability to control your emotions when it counts will play a major a role in your success. Strong feelings of anger, jealousy, exuberance, despair, and others have the power to interfere with your ability to think clearly and make good decisions. The key to control is placing them in psychological compartments, which means blocking them out temporarily so you can focus on the core of what's being said or done so you can respond appropriately. At Mental Toughness University, we call this "The Presidential Problem Solving Technique." The premise is that the President of the United States has a briefing every morning with his cabinet to update him on the most pressing problems that the country is facing around the world. One can only imagine how overwhelming this experience must be for any President. The question is how he is able to deal with multiple life and death decisions all at the same time? The answer is he doesn't. What he does is compartmentalize each problem, and subsequently, handles them one at a time. If he attempted to fix all issues at once, he would quickly become emotionally overwhelmed. Compartmentalizing is essential to becoming rich and successful, so this is something you will need to master. The good news is it's something you can practice at school and at home. The process is simple: all you do is focus on one thing at a time, whether it's on a subject at school, a person you're speaking to or an assignment you're completing. The goal is to see how long you can concentrate on a single subject before your mind begins to wander. The more you practice, the easier it will become and the longer you'll be able to maintain your focus. Do this everyday and notice how you're improving, and make a mental note of how scattered other people appear to you. You'll see why so many people find it difficult to concentrate on any one thing for even a short period of time.

QUOTE:

"I would compartmentalize the industry for the same reason you compartmentalize ships. If you have a leak, the leak doesn't spread and sink the whole vessel." —Warren Buffet

ACTION STEP:

Identify the biggest challenge you're currently facing and compartmentalize it, so it doesn't affect your sense of happiness.

CRITICAL THINKING QUESTION:

On a scale of 1-7, 7 being best, how competent are you are at compartmentalization?

MILLIONAIRE RESOURCE:

Emotional Intelligence Mastery, by Ryan James

CHAPTER 109

Be Congruent

Congruence between your words and actions are critical to your success. You must do what you say you're going to do. On your road to wealth, you're going to encounter many people who talk big and act small. Their words are impressive, but when it comes time to back them up, they fall short. Unfortunately, this is true for most of the population. The reason is that it's easier to mouth off about something than it is to actually make it happen. So the average person bolsters their ego through big talk but takes little action to support their words. This is not a habit you can afford. The key is to get started now by doing everything you say you'll do, and that includes the little things. If you promise Mom that you'll take out the trash by 6pm, make sure it's finished on time. When you tell your teacher you will complete extra homework over the weekend, make sure you complete it. Once you adopt the concept of congruency, people will begin to trust you. And when people trust you, your stock in the world rises. Congruence breeds credibility and credibility creates your reputation. Begin to notice how the people around you make promises they don't keep. Sometimes this is unavoidable, but most times congruency is simply not convenient. Make a note of the different scenarios, and estimate the percentage of people that fulfill their promises. What you'll find is it's a small percentage of people. As strange as it sounds, this is good for you, because their lack of congruence makes your congruence even more impressive. This is another tool that will help you pull away from the masses and elevate you to the world class.

QUOTE:

"Integrity means congruence. Words and behavior match."—Dr. Nathaniel Branden

ACTION STEP:

For the next 7 days, keep track of what you promise and corresponding actions.

CRITICAL THINKING QUESTION:

What percentage of the time do you fulfill your promises?

MILLIONAIRE RESOURCE:

Read: Have a New Teenager by Friday, Dr. Kevin Leman

CHAPTER 110

Avoid Revenge

Beginning in childhood, both at school and in other settings, you will be wronged and cheated. Some of these people will be caught and punished while others will escape justice. Your natural tendency will be to seek revenge and strike back at the perpetrator. This is what average people do to make themselves feel better, but you are not being groomed to be average. Your destiny is to join the ranks of the richest, most successful people in the world, and that means carefully considering every action you take and the consequences, both intended and unintended. The driver who gets cut off in traffic wants revenge, so a mile down the road he cuts off the same driver, accidentally causing a collision that kills his own 2-year old son seated in the passenger's seat. This is an example of an unintended consequence of revenge. The level of consciousness in which the act of revenge takes place is rooted in fear, loss, and hatred, which is a level you want to avoid at all costs. Only on rare occasions does any good or satisfaction ever result from an act of revenge, even though at the time of conception, it seems like a good idea. As a critical thinker, you must come to terms with the fact that sometimes life isn't fair, and unlike your favorite Hollywood movies, sometimes the bad guy gets away. This is just one of the realities of life, and your job is to respond to it in a way that serves your long-term interests. The highest-level response is usually no response at all, at least not directly to the perpetrator. The only response necessary in most situations is the one you offer yourself, which should be to recognize that everyone, including your nemesis, is making decisions at his current level of awareness. And since most people are operating a low level rooted in fear, it's easy to see why they make poor, short-term choices that hurt them in the long run. The cheater might get away, but the fear that drove his behavior will not diminish until he raises his level of thinking. No act of revenge will cause this to happen, so your best bet is to make peace with yourself by letting it go and moving on.

QUOTE:

"Before you embark on a journey of revenge, dig two graves."—Confucius

ACTION STEP:

Forgive the last person that hurt you.

CRITICAL THINKING QUESTION:

Is revenge about settling a score or defending a fragile ego?

MILLIONAIRE RESOURCE:

Read: Radical Forgiveness, by Colin Tipping

CHAPTER 111

Practice Ferocious Cooperation

Being ferociously cooperative means doing everything you can to work well with others. Sometimes you'll be tempted in school to work alone when you're supposed to be working in a group, and this is something you need to avoid. As an aspiring self–made millionaire, you must learn to cooperate. While there is nothing wrong with working independently, the big wins in life usually result from the work of a team. You can't do everything yourself, which means you have to get comfortable getting work done through other people. In school, this begins with your teachers. While some of your classmates may rebel against your teachers, you must be ferociously cooperative and help out in every way you can. Teaching is a tough job. The hours are long, and the pay is small. Every bit of assistance you offer your teachers will be appreciated, and they will cooperate with you when you need them most. Cooperation is how the human race has survived for over 100,000 years. During your school years, teachers hold a powerful position and will play an integral role in your education; therefore it serves your best interests to go above and beyond the normal level of cooperation in your interactions with them. Some kids will call you a "teacher's pet." That's another example of the low-level thinking of the average person, so you should treat it as such and dismiss it. Keep in mind that at various points in your academic career you're going to need help from your teachers, and they will remember your ferocious cooperation when you reach out to them for assistance. Good or bad, right or wrong, this is the way the world works.

QUOTE:

"What works in the real world is cooperation." —Bill Clinton

ACTION STEP:

Offer your cooperation to one of your teachers.

CRITICAL THINKING QUESTION:

On a scale of 1-7, 7 being most cooperative, how cooperative are you?

MILLIONAIRE RESOURCE:

Read: The Evolution of Cooperation, by Robert Axelrod

CHAPTER 112

Avoid Approval Addiction

Psychologists say that the addiction to the approval of other people begins in infancy, and remains with most of us our entire our lives. We learn as infants that if we get the approval from '"the big people," they will give us what we want, and it works. We continue this strategy throughout our childhood and teenage years, and by the time we turn 21, most of us are full blown addicts. Approval addiction is one of the most debilitating of all addictions, mainly because we don't even know that we have it. So we do as we are expected, which often includes career and even whom we marry. When we break away from what is expected, the disapproval we experience can cause us to become demotivated, disempowered and depressed. We feel physical, mental and emotional pain, and often times this is enough to drive us to abandon our own goals and dreams in turn for a safer route that meets others approval. The only known psychological antidote for Approval Addiction is a process known as *Systematic Desensitization*, which is the consistent exposure to disapproval for the purpose of eventually becoming emotionally desensitized. The good news is that your parents are in your corner; otherwise, you probably wouldn't be studying this book. The bad news is you're probably addicted to other people's approval, and you can use the process of Systematic Desensitization to overcome it. When you're a young adult, you must do as you're told, but when you come of age, your goal should be to live life on your own terms, no matter what others think. If they like it, great, and if they don't, well, that's their decision, which has nothing to do with you. Once you break free from the chains of Approval Addiction, your life will open to every dream you ever imagined.

QUOTE:

"The greatest prison people live in, is the fear of what other people think."

ACTION STEP:

Make a list of the 10 people from which you're trying to gain approval.

CRITICAL THINKING QUESTION:

On a scale of 1-7, 7 being most addicted, how addicted are you to the approval of others?

MILLIONAIRE RESOURCE:

Visit Coaching Approval Addiction at www.SieboldNetwork.com

CHAPTER 113

Be Happily Dissatisfied

Life is a series of highs and lows, ups and downs, successes and failures. Your best experiences can become your worst, and your darkest nightmares can turn into your greatest joys. Life is a paradox, and we all experience the rollercoaster of emotion that follows its twists and turns. Most people are happy when life is going well and unhappy when it's not. They simply react to whatever life hands them at the moment, which sets them up as victors or victims of their own circumstances. As an aspiring world-class thinker, this is not a strategy you want to adopt. The best thinkers occupy a psychological space they call being "Happily Dissatisfied." This means they've made a conscious decision to be happy, whether life is going their way or not. They are happy just to be alive, and they guarantee their happiness with the gratitude they feel for everything they have. A common practice among elite performers is listing the things they are grateful for every morning when they wake up and keeping these things in the fronts of their minds during each day, whether life is going their way or not. The "Dissatisfied" part of their philosophy refers to the idea that they are capable of much more than they've demonstrated, and they're always passionately pursuing the next level of success. This is a brilliant personal philosophy you'll want to adopt immediately because it empowers you to operate from a state of happiness while simultaneously recognizing that you are dissatisfied with your current lot in life. This puts you in full control of your emotions and sets you up for consistent and never-ending improvement. Being "Happily Dissatisfied" is a lifelong philosophy that never changes, no matter how successful you become.

QUOTE:

"Be dissatisfied enough to improve, but satisfied enough to be happy."
—J. Harold Smith

ACTION STEP:

Write down 5 people in your life for which you are grateful?

CRITICAL THINKING QUESTION:

In which areas of your life are you "Happily Dissatisfied"?

MILLIONAIRE RESOURCE:

Read: The Science of Happiness, by the Editors of TIME

CHAPTER 114

Learn to Suffer

You are one of the luckiest kids alive. Not only were you born in a rich country loaded with opportunity, but also your parents are highly educated people (either formally, informally, or both) and have made it their mission to prepare you for financial success. You may not realize this now, but as you move into the world, you'll discover that you are literally one in a million people with this level of good fortune. The opportunity to which you are being prepared for is something most people only see in movies. This is your life, and now it's your job to take full advantage of it. The upside of this is success, wealth, and happiness. The downside is you're going to have to fight for it. That means you're going to have to learn how to suffer through the struggle that's required of anyone presented with this type of opportunity. Learning how to suffer means learning how to endure pain, mostly psychological and emotional, and sometimes even physical. When most of your friends are goofing off and having fun, you'll be studying, working and setting goals for the future. When they are spending weekends going to parties, you'll be preparing for your opportunity. Does this mean you can't participate in your adolescence? No. No one wants to take that away from you. That being said, you'll be asked to exercise a higher level of discipline than most of your friends to ensure that you're on track to a life of remarkable success. Sometimes the discipline you'll be asked to employ will be light, and other times it will be a little more. The toughest will be when you have to choose between two alternatives, and while you'll want to choose the fun one, you'll need to choose the one that moves you closer to your goals. This is when sacrifice turns into suffering. Maybe it's missing the High School football game to study for a test. Maybe it's turning away from alcohol at a party. Or maybe it's breaking away from friends who are a bad influence on you. Some of these sacrifices will upset you temporally, and that's why you must learn to endure the pain to secure your long-term best interests. The first step to learning how to suffer is recognizing that sometimes you will feel conflicted and upset along your path to success. The rest of the steps are learned as they are happening. The main takeaway is to remember that successful people are willing to suffer for the long-term payoff while average people refuse to suffer for success unless they are forced. This one distinction between these two groups explains why one of them struggles while the other prospers.

QUOTE:

"Without pain and suffering, we would be nothing"—Brad Pitt

ACTION STEP:

Identify three successes for which you are willing to suffer.

CRITICAL THINKING QUESTION:

Which of your successes in life have you suffered for the most?

MILLIONAIRE RESOURCE:

Read: Super Survivors: The Surprising Link Between Suffering and Success, by David B. Feldman, Ph.D. and Lee Daniel Kravetz

CHAPTER 115

Copy Genius

Most scientists agree that human beings have existed for at least 100,000 years, and during that time our race has bred its share of geniuses. We invented the wheel, the radio and even the Internet over the duration of our history. Considering our humble origins, we have an impressive track record.

This is why you'll want to consider copying genius as opposed to investing substantial amounts of time creating new solutions to current problems. This doesn't mean you should shy away from your own creative, innovative thinking. It just means it will serve your best interests to see if you can copy, in whole or part, solutions from the brilliant people of the past. This will save you time, money and other resources required to create fresh solutions from scratch. The best way to learn about the geniuses of the past is to study them, which is why the self-made rich read biographies of world-class performers. The things you'll learn may offer direct solutions to problems you can get paid to solve, or they may simply offer a way of thinking that leads to your own solution. Great performers process problems in a very different way than the average person and many of them follow their own unique philosophy that guides them. The more of these philosophies you study, the more choices you'll have when forming your own. You may end up copying someone's philosophy directly, or you may decide to blend parts and pieces of a number of them. The key is to study them and draw your own conclusions. Once you do, you'll be starting your career by standing on the shoulders of the giants of the past, which is a strategic advantage few people capitalize on.

QUOTE:

"Copy genius. You'll never live long enough to learn it all on your own."
—Walter Hailey

ACTION STEP:

Ask one of your teachers in school to give you her 3 best tips for becoming a better student.

CRITICAL THINKING QUESTION:

Are you copying genius or attempting to reinvent the wheel?

MILLIONAIRE RESOURCE:

Read: Million Dollar Habits, by Stellan Moreira

CHAPTER 116

Trust Yourself

As you come of age, and throughout your life, you'll to be asked to trust people. As you become successful, you're going to have lots of people who want things from you. Some of them will be trust worthy, others won't. You'll have to use your best judgment to determine which is which, but sometimes you will be wrong. That's life. Build your faith in the trustworthy, and disassociate from the others. Above all, the person you must trust the most is yourself. Trust that you can create the life you want, on your terms. Trust yourself to know when to change course when you're moving in the wrong direction. Trust yourself to know what serves your best interests, and what doesn't. And maybe most importantly, trust that you have the ability and mental toughness to handle anything that life throws at you. Now, you may be thinking that all these things are obvious and that all adults must have this level of self-trust. And in a perfect world, you'd be right. But it's not a perfect world, and most adults don't have the confidence in themselves that they need to thrive and get ahead. They have enough to survive, but that's about it. They've never had the kind of training you're getting here, and after making a series of poor choices in their lives, they lost trust in themselves. Unfortunately, this usually lasts a lifetime. So instead of reaching for their dreams, they play it safe and allow life to pass them by. The sad thing is that most of these people are smart, educated and talented. They can live the life they really want, but the fear they feel from their lack of self-trust forces them to draw back, like a turtle retreating back into his shell. The final thing I want you to know about trusting yourself is that you are going to be wrong sometimes, and the mistakes you make may be costly. Whatever happens, never stop trusting yourself and your own instincts. Everyone makes mistakes, but few people have the self-trust to bounce back. This won't be easy, but it's something you will need to master.

QUOTE:

"Think for yourself. Trust your intuition. Another's mind isn't walking your journey, you are." —Scottie Waves

ACTION STEP:

Identify something you're anxious about, and make a decision to trust yourself to solve it, handle it, or live with it.

CRITICAL THINKING QUESTION:

On a scale of 1-7, 7 being most, how much do you trust yourself?

MILLIONAIRE RESOURCE:

Read: Self Trust, by A.G. Allure

CHAPTER 117

Learn to Sell

Selling is the highest paid profession in the world. The masses often look down on sales people, because they've experienced high-pressure tactics from amateurs. While there are a lot of lousy salespeople, the professionals are to be greatly admired. Nothing happens in the economy until a salesperson sells something, and then a host of sales support people go to work to fulfill the salesperson's promise. No matter what profession you choose to pursue, you need to learn how to sell. Everyone is selling something, all of the time, whether it's products and services, or ideas and philosop. To live is to sell, and the more skill you develop, the more successful you will be. The fact is that people love to buy; so when done correctly, selling is a natural process. The heart of selling involves asking targeted questions to determine if what you offer matches your prospects needs. If it does, the sales process flows smoothly. If what you're selling is not a match for the buyer's needs, then you move on to a better prospect. And that's 90% of the process. Your job is to study the remaining 10%, and then master it. This means reading books on selling, listening to recordings, watching videos, attending seminars and even acquiring a mentor. Every minute you invest learning about selling will pay off in profits for the rest of your life. Start today by asking your parents to help you select a book on selling that will help get you moving in the right direction. Even if you only read one page per day, you will begin to develop a deep understanding of the power and skill of professional selling. Your study will help you build respect for the men and women that lead the professional selling industry. They are smart, tough and persistent, and those are three of the most important skills you can possess on your way to world-class success.

QUOTE:

"We are all salesman everyday of our lives. We are selling our ideas, our plans, our enthusiasm to those with whom we come into contact."
—Charles R. Schwab

ACTION STEP:

List three products or services you would enjoy selling.

CRITICAL THINKING QUESTION:

Who is the best salesperson you've ever met, and why?

MILLIONAIRE RESOURCE:

Read: How I Raised Myself from Failure to Success in Selling, by Frank Bettger

CHAPTER 118

Simplify Everything

Life is complex. The world is complex. People are complex. While it's difficult to debate these realities, your job is to simplify everything you can and focus on what's important. Decide what you want, concentrate on it to the exclusion of (almost) everything else, and embrace the challenge of attaining it. Determine where you fit into the world, and you'll find happiness. Learn what the people you love care about most, and give it to them if you can. If you are unable to do so, help them move towards it. One of the secrets of world-class thinking is taking complex problems and breaking them down into simple solutions. Disassembling a car engine is complicated, but if you take it apart one piece at a time, it's simple. Deciding what you want to do for a living is difficult, but if you pay attention to which subjects you naturally gravitate towards, your passion will guide you. People's emotions can be complex, but each one has a root. The jilted lover, feeling heartbroken, is actually experiencing betrayal and loss. The child who is angry with his father for leaving the family is experiencing feelings of abandonment. The employee who gets fired unfairly is experiencing feelings of disloyalty. The point is everything can be broken down to its root cause, and that makes every problem easier to solve.

QUOTE:

"Simplicity is the ultimate sophistication."—Leonardo Da Vinci

ACTION STEP:

Break down, in the simplest terms, your strengths and weaknesses in school.

CRITICAL THINKING QUESTION:

What are the three most important study habits of the best students in your class?

MILLIONAIRE RESOURCE:

Read: Simple Thinking: How to Remove Complexity from Life and Work, by Richard Gerver

CHAPTER 119

Develop Courage

Staking your own claim requires courage. It goes against the grain of society, even in America, where we celebrate our entrepreneurial heroes. Most people have neither the desire nor the ambition to chart their own course in life, so they choose to follow those that do. Your journey to success and riches begins now, as you're learning how the world works and the secrets to navigating it successfully. Once you've achieved world-class success, which you will certainly do, the masses will hold you in high regard. Success is hard to argue against. It's in the early stages of the process that requires great personal courage because that's when people see you attempting to ascend to a level of success they don't want you to reach. Some people will be supportive as you claw your way upward, while others may laugh and criticize your audacious aspirations. This is where courage kicks in, and you get to see what you're made of. Does the limited, fear-based thinking of the middle class disempower you, or does it strengthen your resolve? Do you long to fit in, or have you made peace with the fact that you are different? It's easy to go with the crowd and seek acceptance, but it takes guts to break away from the masses knowing that they will punish you. Remember that extraordinary success requires original thinking, behavior, and action. Sometimes this means sacrificing popularity to give you the best chance of succeeding. This begins right now, today when you are still in school. The other kids may make fun of you for sitting in the front row in class, asking the teacher questions and engaging in class discussions. They may mock you for helping and supporting your teachers. They may not understand when you ask for extra credit assignments. Remember when they are rejecting you that they represent the mass consciousness, and they will likely stay there their entire lives. You are being groomed for greatness, and that requires the courage to embrace the world-class methodology of success.

QUOTE:

"Courage is being scared to death… And saddling up anyway."—John Wayne

ACTION STEP:

During the next week, do something you're afraid to do and monitor your feelings in the process.

CRITICAL THINKING QUESTION:

If you develop twice as much courage as you have now, how might your life be different?

MILLIONAIRE RESOURCE:

Read: Courage to Soar, by Simone Biles

CHAPTER 120

Become a Learning Machine

Learning and growing are the essences of the good life. It means you are always moving forward and never looking back. Studies show that most people stop reading after high school or college. This is clearly not the direction you want to travel. Graduation from your school, which will be your *formal* education, kicks off your informal education, which lasts a lifetime. The centerpiece of your education should be reading, listening and watching educational programming, attending personal and professional development seminars and workshops, studying with mentors, traveling the world and becoming a student observer of success, life, and living. In short, you need to become a learning machine that is continually searching for answers, explanations, and new distinctions in thinking. While the masses are more interested in entertaining themselves, your focus needs to be on educating yourself. The more you know, the more of life opens up to you. The world is a fascinating place to discover, full of wonder and mystery. The more well rounded you become through education, the more you will understand and enjoy it. Social education will help you build healthy relationships. Historical knowledge will help you understand the world. Political education will assist you in navigating laws and regulations. And financial education will make you rich. Studying painting, music, dance and other art forms will add a deeper dimension to your life and make it even more enjoyable. But above and beyond all the things you will learn, will be the personal growth and satisfaction you will experience in the process of becoming better tomorrow than you are today. You will carry that deep sense of fulfillment with you for the rest of your life, and no one will ever be able to take it away. Start today by making a commitment to become an outstanding student in school, and then select a subject outside of your formal studies that you would like to learn more about. This multifaceted approach to education will serve you for the rest of your life.

QUOTE:

"You cannot fail, you can only learn and grow" —Larry Wilson

ACTION STEP:

Add a new dimension to your life by learning a musical instrument, writing poetry, painting or anything else that helps you discover fresh ways of seeing things.

CRITICAL THINKING QUESTION:

How can you increase your appetite for learning?

MILLIONAIRE RESOURCE:

Read: The Success Principles for Teens: How To Get From Where You Are to Where You Want to Be, by Jack Canfield and Kent Healy

CHAPTER 121

Program Yourself Through Self-Talk

Contrary to what others will tell you, the most important conversations you will ever have will be with yourself. What you say when you talk to yourself will form the nucleus of your belief system, and your habits, actions, and behaviors will be a reflection of your beliefs. Studies show that 77% of what most people say when they talk to themselves is negative, fear-based and disempowering, which becomes the central theme of their mediocrity. The emotional nature of human being's makes us highly susceptible to persistent messaging, whether it be positive and empowering or negative and disempowering. Human Beings can be programmed, or brainwashed, to believe almost anything. This includes mysticism, astrology, and fairy tales. This is how religious cults like Scientology, Heavens Gate, and The Branch Davidians have successfully brainwashed people to believe the unbelievable. The followers of these cults aren't stupid; they are simply the victims of consistent, strategic brainwashing. While these examples represent the dark side of psychological programming, it can also be used to build your mind into a high performance success machine. Repeating positive, empowering success-driven messages to yourself has the power to drive your behaviors like nothing else. The secret is to monitor everything you're saying to yourself and guard the door of your mind against any words that threaten to erode your confidence or damage your self-image. Start by telling yourself how goal oriented, ambitious and focused you are every day. Tell yourself that you are a highly disciplined, success-seeking machine that never quits. Tell yourself that you always go the extra mile to succeed, whether it's in class, completing homework assignments or performing chores around the house. You always do quality work, even if you don't enjoy it. Tell yourself that you're a winner and that winners always do the right things in the right way with the right attitude. The more positive, success oriented language you use to talk to yourself, the stronger you will become and the faster your words will reflect reality. Oh, and don't expect the masses to understand the power of this principle. Most of them won't believe it and will refuse to even try it.

QUOTE:

"Self-talk is the most powerful form of communication because it either empowers you or it defeats you."

ACTION STEP:

Start telling yourself everyday that you are destined to become a self-made millionaire.

CRITICAL THINKING QUESTION:

If you improved the quality and quantity of your positive self-talk, would you be a better, happier more fulfilled student?

MILLIONAIRE RESOURCE:

Listen to The Making of a Million Dollar Mind, by Steve Siebold, at www.MillionDollarMind.com

CHAPTER 122

Take Responsibility

You are responsible for your own success, fulfillment, and happiness. Regardless of what you hear from middle-class thinkers, your highest purpose in life is to fulfill your own potential and accept full responsibility for your successes and failures. You'll hear the masses blame everyone but themselves for their struggles, from government, teachers and even their parents. It's never their fault because they refuse to grow up and accept the fact that they are the makers of their own destinies. Difficult circumstances, bad breaks and freak accidents occur in most peoples lives, but the mentally tough winners are able to shake off the struggle and get back on track to their goals and dreams. They're not waiting for a hero on a white horse to ride in and save them—*they* are the heroes, and they know they are 100% responsible for saving themselves. See it's easier to abdicate responsibility because it gives you someone to blame when you fail. It's the method people use to let themselves off the hook. Taking responsibility means facing life head on, with no excuses or apologies. It means accepting yourself; warts and all, and working to improve everyday. It's realizing that none of us are perfect, and we all make mistakes. Refuse to allow anyone to tell you that you're responsible for others. It's not your job to fight anyone else's battle. Everyone is responsible for his or her own success, fulfillment and happiness. It's not your job to save the world. Focus on your own success, and when you reach the point where you're comfortable, you'll have the opportunity to help as many people as you wish. Don't buy into the altruistic notion that you should place other peoples needs above your own. Take responsibility for your own life first, and become a role model for others to do the same. The best way you can help the poor, middle class and the struggling is not to become one of them.

QUOTE:

"In the long run, we shape our lives, and we shape ourselves. The process never ends until we die. And the choices we make are ultimately our own responsibility." —Eleanor Roosevelt

ACTION STEP:

From this day forward, take full responsibility for every grade you receive in school.

CRITICAL THINKING QUESTION:

In what area of your life have you not accepted 100% responsibility?

MILLIONAIRE RESOURCE:

Read: Taking Responsibility: Self-Reliance and the Accountable Life, by Nathaniel Branden, Ph.D.

CHAPTER 123

Wield Your Power Carefully

You are going to be rich and powerful. People are going to admire and emulate you. You're going to influence people's lives through your success. While all of this is a wonderful position to hold, it comes with responsibilities. The most important being how you use your influence and power. Your choices are simple: use your success to control, manipulate and enslave people or to empower them. Due to your success, every word you speak is magnified in the minds of people who look up to you. They will hang on everything you say as if it were being handed down from the heavens. You must discipline yourself to be acutely aware of everything you say and do because the negative impact of saying the wrong thing to the wrong person could alter the course of their lives. There's an old saying; "If you want to see the true character of a man, give him power." While some axioms are better than others, this one is accurate. People driven by power love to lord it over others. That's the opposite of what you want to do. Follow the Golden Rule: "treat people the way you want to be treated." Be nice. Be thoughtful, and be yourself. This is not only a solid business strategy; it's the right thing to do. The abuse of power is the shameful act of a bully. It hurts and disempowers people. Power is a great thing to have, but like owning a gun, it must only be used when all other options have been exhausted. Discipline yourself not to use your position, money or power to influence other people's behavior unless it's absolutely necessary. If you do this, you'll have a greater level of respect for yourself and others will admire your restraint.

QUOTE:

“Nearly all men can stand adversity, but if you want to test a mans character, give him power.” —Abraham Lincoln

ACTION STEP:

Begin to notice how people with power use it.

CRITICAL THINKING QUESTION:

Do you believe having power will change you for better or worse?

MILLIONAIRE RESOURCE:

Read: The 48 Laws of Power, by Robert Green

CHAPTER 124

Embrace Conflict

The masses avoid conflict. They hate it. But the truth is that constructive conflict can be a valuable learning mechanism. When smart people disagree on ideas, philosophies and strategies, new levels of understanding can be reached. The reason most people abhor conflict is that they allow their emotions to cloud their judgment. This leads them to see the conflict as a personal assault, both on themselves and their ideas. The cost of this emotional intrusion is the possible loss of knowledge, awareness and new distinctions in thinking. As you grow up, you'll hear people say that you should never discuss sex, politics or religion in mixed company. Many teachers and authorities claim that discussions and debates on these subjects are impolite and inappropriate. This is due to the emotional immaturity of the average person who is incapable of containing and controlling their emotions when it comes to hearing an opposing viewpoint. Instead, teachers, coaches, clergy, and other adults of influence will tell you to stick to less controversial topics such as sports, weather, and entertainment. The problem with this approach is that you lose the opportunity to learn and grow from other people's perspectives on issues that actually matter. Constructive conflict requires an emotional maturity that most people don't have, so your job is to choose friends that have it or are capable of acquiring it. Once you find them, challenge their ideas on important topics and ask them to challenge yours. Together, you'll reach new levels of understanding, and you'll become smarter and more educated. This is the strategy world-class thinkers use to solve societies most pressing problems. On your own, you are capable of great things, but when you join forces with other smart, educated people, almost anything is possible.

QUOTE:

"Conflict is inevitable, but combat is optional." —Max Lucado

ACTION STEP:

The next time you enter a conflict, lower your voice and soften your tone to disarm your opponent.

CRITICAL THINKING QUESTION:

Is conflict more about differences in opinion or ego?

MILLIONAIRE RESOURCE:

Read: The innovation Code: The Creative Power of Constructive Conflict, by Jeff DeGraff and Staney DeGraff

CHAPTER 125

Raise Your Expectations

Many psychologists believe that people should lower their expectations, so they won't be disappointed if they fail. They believe people will be happier expecting and settling for less. This is another mass oriented formula for failure. You'll usually get what you expect, and *rarely* get more than you expect. Is it possible to set high expectations and fall short? Yes. Sometimes giving it everything you have isn't enough. Failure is a part of life. But winners don't avoid, ignore or run away from reality. They embrace it. Instead of being frightened by the facts of life, they look them squarely in the eye. Winners don't live in fear; they live in a world of possibilities, potential, and opportunity. They know if they set high expectations for their lives that they may fall short and be disappointed. That's life. No one likes to believe it will happen, but sometimes it does. This isn't Hollywood; this is real life, where the good guy doesn't always get the girl. Every time you raise your expectations, you run the risk of reaching higher than you're capable of climbing. That's ok. Raise your expectations anyway. Let the middle class be satisfied with mediocrity while you reach for the stars. The only way you'll know if your overreaching is by trying, and the only downside to trying is the possibility of being disappointed. That's where mental toughness kicks in. The irony of it all is that facing fear head on is the easiest way to reduce its power. Once you stare it down and accept the consequences, it no longer controls your life. The most extreme example you'll witness is how the masses approach their ultimate fear, the fear of death. How do they face it? They don't. Instead, they focus on their next life in the hereafter, so they don't have to deal with the reality of dying. And because they are so afraid of dying, they are even more afraid of living. This is not for you. Reject fear, expect to live your dreams, and accept the realities of life with mental toughness.

QUOTE:

"Expect more from yourself than others."

ACTION STEP:

Raise your expectations for yourself and lower them for others.

CRITICAL THINKING QUESTION:

Are the expectations you have for your life high enough to match your ambition and talent?

MILLIONAIRE RESOURCE:

Read: The 7 Habits of Highly Effective Teens, by Sean Covey

CHAPTER 126

Know That Money has Limits

You're going to be rich, but you need to know that while money is an important part of life, it's not *everything*. There's a limit to how much fun and happiness you can buy. Many people use this as an excuse for not becoming wealthy. This is a naïve philosophy that leaves millions who have the opportunity struggling to survive. Being rich is more about controlling your own life than it is about material purchases. After all, you can only live in one house, drive one car, and eat one steak at a time. People dream of getting rich so they can indulge themselves in all of their hearts desires, only to realize when they do that it isn't nearly as fulfilling as they expected. It's nice to have beautiful things, and you will have plenty. The best benefit, besides controlling your life, is never having to worry about how you are going to pay your bills. Being rich eliminates stress in which the poor and middle class are saddled. After that, your next level of happiness will come from things not related to money at all. These are the things that money can't buy, like loving relationships, fulfilling work, and the simple joy of living. Most of your happiness in life will come from these non-monetary areas. Money can only take you so far, but without it, you're facing a lifetime of stress and struggle. The people that claim that money doesn't matter are kidding themselves, and the people that think getting rich is going to make them happy are doing the same thing. Be happy now, no matter what you do or don't have. Being happy is not so much a state of mind as it is a decision that you make for yourself. Decide to be happy as you continue to strive for your goals, and remember to build loving relationships along the way to ensure your long-term happiness.

QUOTE:

"Money is numbers and numbers never end. If it takes money to be happy, your search for happiness will never end." —Bob Marley

ACTION STEP:

Think of the last material possession you wanted, and how long it made you happy after you got it.

CRITICAL THINKING QUESTION:

Is money more about materialism or control?

MILLIONAIRE RESOURCE:

Read: Happiness: A Guide to Developing Life's Most Important Skill, by Matthieu Ricard

CHAPTER 127

Use Enthusiasm and Momentum

One of the secrets of success is knowing how to control and manipulate your emotions to serve your best interests. This is the definition of mental toughness. Humans are emotional beings *that know* they are emotional beings. In essence, we are machines that know we are machines, and the key to your success will be learning how to operate your machine at maximum efficiency. This means identifying the thoughts, habits, actions, and behaviors that create emotional enthusiasm and momentum. When you're enthusiastic about your work you're going to be at your best, and when you're at your best day after day, it creates emotional momentum. Once you have momentum on your side, you become unstoppable. The things that normally slow you down disappear. Stumbling blocks turn into stepping stones, and you experience this overwhelming feeling that you cannot be defeated. Eventually, these feelings turn into rock solid beliefs, and become a self-fulfilling prophecy. You feel strong, courageous and bold, like a freight train thundering down a track. This puts you in a high-energy vibration that others can feel, like an excited child opening her toys on Christmas morning. Your energy is infectious, and people want to be around you just to bathe in it. People that previously said no to you; start saying yes, and you'll feel like you can accomplish anything you desire. If this sounds like magic, it is. It's the magic of an emotional machine that's being controlled and manipulated by its master. This is the primary reason that your success is in your hands. The more you learn about your machines hot buttons and motivators, the more it (you) will produce. Start doing this in school and see what happens. Notice how your teachers and fellow students respond to you. Most people won't understand the significance of what you're doing, including your teachers. It doesn't matter. Your job is to begin practicing being enthusiastic and to quietly observe how your emotional momentum begins to grow.

QUOTE:

"Success is the ability to go from failure to failure without losing your enthusiasm." —Winston Churchill

ACTION STEP:

Check your level of enthusiasm every day and talk to yourself in ways that will increase it.

CRITICAL THINKING QUESTION:

On a scale of 1-7, 7 being most enthusiastic, how would you rate yourself?

MILLIONAIRE RESOURCE:

Read: Hustle: The Power to Charge Your Life with Money, Meaning and Momentum, by Neil Patel, Patrick Vlaskovits and Jonas Koffler

CHAPTER 128

Learn to Cope with Criticism

As an aspiring self-made millionaire, you are in the minority. That means you're going to be ridiculed and criticized. The masses rarely understand the inner workings of world-class thinkers, and instead of trying to learn, they often choose to criticize and condemn. Don't allow this to bother you, and don't waste your energy trying to change it. The middle class, mediocre mindset is a disease. When inferior thinkers begin to ridicule your actions, you'll know you're on the right track. Sounds twisted, I know. But that's how it's always been. There's a great psychological divide between producers like you and people that simply feed off of the producer's effort. You might call these two groups, the "Makers and the Takers." Being a "Maker" always seems to draw criticism from the "Takers" even though these are the people that supply the jobs, products and services that keep them alive. Seems self-destructive, right? It is, but I think deep down the "Takers" know that the "Makers" will not stop producing, no matter how much criticism with which they are bombarded. Learning to cope with criticism is a process known as "Systematic Desensitization." In essence, it's the process of hearing criticism so many times for so long that you eventually desensitize from the pain it initially causes. Once you desensitize, experiencing criticism is no more than a nuisance, like swatting a fly. It just doesn't matter anymore, and that's the point you have to reach so it loses the power to slow you down. The single exception to ignoring criticism is when you believe it has merit and you might learn from it. The key is to keep an open mind and consider each criticism as potentially valuable.

QUOTE:

"Learn to take criticism seriously, but not personally." —Hillary Clinton

ACTION STEP:

Begin to evaluate criticism more seriously and see if you can learn from it.

CRITICAL THINKING QUESTION:

The last time you received constructive criticism; did you react negatively or respond positively?

MILLIONAIRE RESOURCE:

Read: Resilience: Facing Down Rejection and Criticism on The Road to Success, by Mark Mcguinness

CHAPTER 129

Focus on Results

There's an old saying: "It's not if you win or lose, its how you play the game." In amateur sports, that saying has real wisdom. In the real world, winning is the key to getting what you want. How you play the game is important; your attitude, ethics, and approach make a difference. Always play fair. But to reap the rewards, you must secure the victory. That's why you must focus on getting results from your actions, starting with your school work. You need to build the habit of getting results, even in subjects you don't enjoy. Your job is to bring excellence to everything you do, from the comments you make in class to the homework you submit to your teacher. You should be known in school as a "results machine." This includes your behavior in after school activities, gym class and even at lunchtime with your friends. When you get known for delivering results, people trust, respect and admire you. The jealous kids might call you a "suck up" for your ferocious cooperation with your teachers, but they will still come to you when they need help. When your parents ask you to do chores around the house, give them results that exceed their expectations. All of this learned behavior will transfer into your daily life, and after a while, it will become a part of who you are. When you begin applying for college, the powers at be will see that you are someone who delivers results and will bring excellence to their institution. After you spend four years of college getting great results, potential employers will see it and will hire you to bring the same results to their company. After you deliver the results to your employer, you will be skilled enough to start your own company and stake your own claim. Remember: talk is cheap, and the world runs on results. Make a decision today to produce results wherever you go, however you can.

QUOTE:

"The results you achieve will be in direct proportion to the effort you apply." —Denis Waitley

ACTION STEP:

Ask your parents and your teachers how you can get better results at home and in school.

CRITICAL THINKING QUESTION:

Are you delivering the results you are capable of?

MILLIONAIRE RESOURCE:

Read: The 6 Most Important Decisions You'll Ever Make, by Sean Covey

CHAPTER 130

Maintain a Sense of Urgency

At this moment you're young, and time moves slow and steady. You'll soon discover that with each passing year, time seems to accelerate. The world operates from a sense of urgency to get things down now, while there's still time, and that's the same way you need to structure your time. This begins with completing class assignments, homework, chores, sports or music practice, and anything else you've committed to in advance or at least on time. The masses do the opposite. They procrastinate, stall and put-off fulfilling their commitments to the very last minute, which is often too late. They refuse to act with any sense of urgency, and their teachers, coaches, parents, and friends all know it. This is another way to separate yourself from the masses and to show the influential people around you that you are serious about success. Maintaining a sense of urgency is a habit, in the same sense that winning is a habit. So is losing and lounging around as though the world will wait for you, which it won't. Urgency is one of the things America is known for as a country. The urgency to invent, innovate and solve problems. While many first world countries are taking it easy and telling us to slow down, we continue to lead the world in business. Our culture is criticized around the globe for being too intense and focused on results, yet we are the richest country in the history of the world. When other countries experience natural disasters and need money, guess whom they call? This is the same with the rich and successful. You will be lambasted for bringing urgency to everything you do, but when the people who criticize you need something done, to whom do you think they will turn? Decide now to become a master of managing your time and people will see you as a leader.

QUOTE:

"Everyone should have a sense of urgency—it is getting a lot done in a short period of time, in a calm, confident manner." —Bob Proctor

ACTION STEP:

CriticaChallenge yourself to treat your homework assignments at school with a sense of urgency.

CRITICAL THINKING QUESTION:

Do you understand the difference between urgency and emergency?

MILLIONAIRE RESOURCE:

Read: The Power of Urgency, by William Keiper

CHAPTER 131

Fight for Your Success

You will enter the business world with the advantage of being groomed, conditioned and prepared for wealth and success. You are being taught things in this book that the majority of your teachers, coaches, clergy and other developers of youth don't fully understand. You've been given the gift of having parents that know how the system works, and that there's a process that the self-made rich follow to achieve their dreams. You have a head start that most people only dream of, and now it's up to you to capitalize on it. The knowledge and strategies you've learned so far are world class, but they won't be enough to carry you to prosperity. You will have to fight the battle every millionaire businessperson fights, and it will be filled with rejection, setbacks, long hours, sacrifice and failure. As you endure and persist in the effort to stake your claim, you will become battle hardened and mentally tough. The obstacles that once stood in your way will fall, and the fear of failure that used to keep you awake at night will disappear. As tempting as it may be to wish the battle was easier, focus instead on how you can become better. The more adversity you face, the stronger you will become, and the stronger you become, the more successful you will be. Becoming a self-made millionaire isn't a sprint; it's a marathon; so prepare yourself for the long haul so you don't tire too quickly. When it gets tough, and you're feeling beat up and frustrated, remember that this isn't supposed to be easy. If it were easy, everyone would be rich. No one can fight this battle for you. You'll have to do this yourself. Armed with the knowledge you now have, being rich is *yours to lose*. The question is; are you willing to fight for it?

QUOTE:

"Victory is always possible for the person who refuses to stop fighting."
—Napoleon Hill

ACTION STEP:

Start fighting for better grades in school.

CRITICAL THINKING QUESTION:

How hard and long are you willing to fight for what you want?

MILLIONAIRE RESOURCE:

Read: Grit: The Power of Passion and Perseverance, by Angela Duckworth

CHAPTER 132

Build a Network of Powerful People

One of the things you'll hear is that it's not just what you know, but whom you know, and there's a lot of truth to that statement. Of course being successful isn't only based on whom you know; it's a combination of being excellent at what you do along with knowing who can help you sell more of it. Make no mistake: to become wealthy in your field of choice, you must be a world-class performer. The masses will have you believe that the system is rigged, and all you have to do to succeed on a massive scale is to know people in powerful positions. It's the average person's excuse for not being successful as if they are actually doing what it takes to make it big. This excuse makes it easier for them to accept their mediocre results. Do not buy into this low-level thinking. Instead, construct the winning combination of developing world-class skills in your profession while simultaneously building a network of powerful people that you can help you. Notice I said "powerful people." The middle-class business person thinks that it's the number of people in their network that counts. It's not. What counts is how "powerful" the people in your network are. Having one president of a successful company in your network is more valuable than having one hundred people that work on an assembly line. Build your network selectively, and it starts in school. This is one of the reasons you need to become an excellent student because top students go to the best colleges and universities. The contacts at Harvard, Yale, and Stanford, are going to be far superior to the contacts at your local community college. The masses hate this fact and call it elitism, but this is the way the world works. While they kick and scream about how unfair life is, you need to be working hard to gain access to people who can help you. Once you graduate, you continue building your network at the places where powerful people go: country clubs, rich neighborhoods, black tie dinners, charity events, golf and tennis clubs, etc. The more you frequent these places and events, the bigger your network of powerful people will grow and the more successful you will become. And then you will become rich and powerful, and people will want to network with you, which will take you even higher.

QUOTE:

"Networking is an essential part of building wealth."—Armstrong Williams

ACTION STEP:

Build relationships with the smartest kids, teachers, and administrators in the school. Keep records of everything you learn about them for the future.

CRITICAL THINKING QUESTION:

How many people do you have in your network?

MILLIONAIRE RESOURCE:

Read: Networking Like a Pro: Turning Contacts into Connections, by Ivan Misner, Ph.D.

CHAPTER 133

Be Bold

The average person is living in fear and struggling to survive even though they are surrounded by opportunity and abundance. Their timidity is evident in their approach to life, and their ultimate goal is to avoid pain. These are smart, talented, well-educated people who have decided to play not to lose instead of playing to win. Deep down they believe that fear protects them from the threats of the world, and they take as few risks as necessary. This is the perfect recipe for mediocrity, and most people achieve it. World-class performers do the exact opposite. They shun fear, act bold and move courageously towards their dreams. This is the only strategy that makes sense. Life is a game with a time clock, and human beings are the only animal on the planet that knows its time is limited. You're born, you live, and you die. That's the reality of life. You get one chance to create your dream life by pursuing your passions, and that requires a bold, aggressive approach. Being bold means fearlessly moving through life with the focus and intention of a tiger seeking its prey. Boldness breeds missteps and mistakes because it moves fast and fearlessly, but it also leads to great achievement. Being bold will draw criticism from the masses, and adulation from the world class. Never worry about the wrath of the masses. Their anger over your actions is rooted in the disappointment they feel in themselves. Being bold starts in school, when you assert yourself as a leader through ferocious cooperation with teachers, students, and school faculty. Become a model student in grades, effort, and attitude, and learn to ignore the backlash you receive from students who don't understand your strategy.

QUOTE:

"Freedom lies in being bold."—Robert Frost

ACTION STEP:

Make a bold move this week by asking the Principal of your school if you can interview him or her on success.

CRITICAL THINKING QUESTION:

On a scale of 1-7, 7 being boldest, how bold have you been in the past?

MILLIONAIRE RESOURCE:

Read: Overcoming Fear: 50 Lessons on Being Bold and Living the Dream, by Joe Serio, Ph.D.

CHAPTER 134

Follow Mentors

One of the success strategies the rich and powerful employ is the engagement of mentors; people who have reached the heights they want to reach and learned the lessons of a lifetime reaching them. Mentors can save you time, money, and heartache. The best ones will hold your hand and guide you step-by-step. Potential mentors are everywhere, and you should begin searching for one right now to help you become an outstanding student. Teachers, tutors, and school faculty are a good place to look. Even if you're a great student, the mentorship of an academic expert will take your success to the next level. When I was in college, I asked my English professor to mentor me, and in one year I went from straight C's to straight A's, and eventually won the Presidential Scholarship Award from the University of South Alabama. My mentor taught me the habits and philosophies of the top students she taught over the past 30 years, and all I did was copy them. Hopefully, you're a better student than I was when you get to college, but even if you're not, a mentor can help you change your academic life. My mentor professor told me that I was the only student in her 30-year career that ever asked her to be a mentor. Interesting, huh? It will probably be the same for you. That's how rare you become when you begin employing world-class thinking. Most kids just want to be liked and accepted by the other students, but the best students want to be liked and accepted by their teachers. While most teachers fall into middle-class thinking as it relates to business and financial success, they are serious experts at what it takes to become a super star student. After you graduate from college, you'll need a new mentor to help guide you in your career of choice. Do your research, select carefully, and ask humbly. And then do everything your mentor tells you to do. The biggest mistake mentees make is questioning or ignoring their mentor's direction, and that's why they lose them. Either follow your mentor or get a new one that you trust and believe in. His or her guidance will thrust you years ahead of your colleagues and competitors.

QUOTE:

"Mentorship is the key to extraordinary success."—Mike Murdock

ACTION STEP:

Ask one of your teachers, counselors, or school faculty to be your academic mentor.

CRITICAL THINKING QUESTION:

If you had an academic mentor, could you become one the best students in your class?

MILLIONAIRE RESOURCE:

Read: The Teenagers Guide to School Outside the Box, by Rebecca Green

CHAPTER 135

Learn to Say No

The more successful you become, the more people will be asking for your time. Their requests will cover a wide range of things; from business deals to donations. Some of these requests will be worth your time and others won't, and you'll have to determine which is which. The good news is, due to your success, you will be presented with new and unique opportunities. The bad news is you will also be presented with things that are a waste of time. Somewhere in the middle there will be requests for charitable giving, and you'll have to decide which groups, if any, you would like to support. It's nice to give back, but you can't give to everyone, so you'll be forced to make choices. The most valuable skill you can possess in this process is the ability to say no. While it sounds easy enough to say those words, it's not quite as simple when someone in need is standing right in front of you begging for help. People don't like to be rejected, and they may voice their displeasure in a manner that makes you feel guilty. This is why you have to develop the mental toughness to ignore unfair criticism, especially from overly emotional people who are searching for a handout. This will begin in school, as you become a top student. There will be a group of struggling students who will attempt to copy your answers on tests; ask you to complete their homework and pepper you with questions after class. You will have to decide who is worthy of your help, and who is not. Just understand that denying people time, money, assistance and anything else doesn't make you a bad or evil person, it simply makes you a person who knows how to manage his time, money and resources. Don't take his or her negative responses personally, as you are under no *obligation* to serve anyone but yourself. Saying no without guilt will be one of the most important skills you will need to learn.

QUOTE:

"You have to decide what your highest priorities are, and have the courage—pleasantly, smilingly, unapologetically—to say 'no' to other things. And the way to do that is by having a bigger 'yes' burning inside.
—Stephen Covey

ACTION STEP:

In the next 7 days, say 'no' to something or someone to free up some of your time.

CRITICAL THINKING QUESTION:

How often do you say yes when you want to say no?

MILLIONAIRE RESOURCE:

Read: Boundaries: When to Say Yes, How to Say No to Take Control of Your Life, by Henry Cloud and John Townsend

CHAPTER 136

Fail Forward

Success is usually built on a series of attempts and failures. Most people view failure as a death sentence for success. So instead of learning from the failure and moving forward, they shrink back to their comfort zones and play it safe for the rest of their lives. The road to riches is paved with missteps, setbacks, and failures. While failure isn't fun, it is the foundation of your education, which eventually will make you rich. Whether you fail to make an "A" on your math test or you lose a million dollars in a deal, the secret is to always fail forward towards your dream. Failing backward means you're losing because you'd rather sit on the couch than go to work. Failing forward means working toward your dream, and every failure moves you closer. Making mistakes, and the education they will give you, is to be expected and embraced. This allows you to begin again, but this time more intelligently.

Past failures make you more aware of what works and what doesn't, and that will give you an advantage as you resume your efforts. Getting a 'B' on an English test isn't bad, but maybe it's not the "A" you expected. Once you dissect the answers you missed, you can focus on correcting them. The girl you asked to the school dance may have said no, but this rejection has mentally prepared you for the next attempt. As long as you continue to ask, you'll get better in your delivery and more confident in yourself. This is what it means to fail forward.

QUOTE:

"The essence of man is imperfection. Failure is simply a price we pay to achieve success. If we learn to embrace that new definition of failure, then we are free to start moving ahead—and failing forward." —Norman Cousins

ACTION STEP:

Ask for something you want, and even if you don't get it, you will fail forward towards it.

CRITICAL THINKING QUESTION:

How does this chapter change the way you see failure?

MILLIONAIRE RESOURCE:

Read: Failing Forward, by John C. Maxwell

CHAPTER 137

Use Solitude

Becoming a great performer isn't easy. Whether it's getting A's in school or amassing a fortune, it takes dedication, strategy, and persistence to win. You're growing up in the instant information age, where anything you want to know is one click away. It's an amazing time that mankind has worked toward for thousands of years. That's the upside. The downside is that information is flowing, growing and expanding so quickly that it can become emotionally overwhelming. This is why you should use solitude as a strategy. Whether it's taking a walk by yourself, relaxing in your room or playing a musical instrument, being alone with your thoughts gives your brain a break from the constant barrage of information. Solitude creates space between thoughts and gives you time to address issues that have real consequences. It's easy to become overwhelmed in a world where everyone wants everything yesterday. The use of a floatation tank, meditation, yoga, martial arts, painting and other forms of eliminating excessive cognition are all underrated and underused. This is fine for the average person, but you're not average, and that means you'll need every high performance strategy you can employ. The harder you push your mind to produce, the more recovery will be required to maintain that level of thinking. Every couple of hours, during high intensity thinking, take a short break to allow your mind to rest and recover. Once you feel refreshed, re-engage back into your work with enthusiasm and persistence. You'll feel more creative, energetic and optimistic. As the day gets longer, you'll need to inject longer periods of solitude to remain at full cognitive capacity. The more you practice being by yourself, the better you will become.

QUOTE:

"Without great solitude, no serious work is possible."—Pablo Picasso

ACTION STEP:

Invest at least 30 minutes per day in quiet solitude.

CRITICAL THINKING QUESTION:

Do you spend enough time alone to allow your mind to calmly consider solutions to your problems?

MILLIONAIRE RESOURCE:

Read: The Book of Floating: Exploring the Private Sea, by Michael Hutchison

CHAPTER 138

Money is Your Friend

The masses see money as a negative, nasty, necessary evil. They fear it, worry about it, and sometimes even die for it. Money has gotten a bad rap because it's misunderstood. The fact is that money is one of the most important aspects of life, as much as most people would like to deny it. As a future self-made millionaire, you need to see money as your friend. This is a friend that offers you opportunity, peace of mind and fun. Money can even save your life. Right or wrong, all doctors and other medical professionals are not equal. Some are better than others, and the best doctors are usually the most expensive. Many of them only accept cash, and even the best medical insurance isn't enough to place them in your employ. You may argue that in the United States of America, it shouldn't be like this. While you may be correct, the fact remains that rich people can travel anywhere in the world to get medical assistance. Drugs that have not been approved by the FDA may be available in other countries. The same goes for medical procedures.

Many people can't afford to travel outside the US for surgery, even if the savings are substantial. Open-heart surgery in the United States may cost $100,000, but in Costa Rica, the same surgery with equally skilled physicians may only cost $20,000. The point is that money will control a most of your life unless you're rich enough to buy your control back. Make money your friend by talking about it positively, regarding what it can do for you and other people. Developing a healthy relationship with money means respecting its power in your life, and seeing it as a medium exchange instead of an indicator of self-worth. Earn lots, spend little, and save and invest as much as you can. If you will, you will control money.If you don't, money will control you.

QUOTE:

"Lack of money is the root of all evil." —George Bernard Shaw

ACTION STEP:

Make three positive statements about money every day.

CRITICAL THINKING QUESTION:

Do you see money as your friend or enemy?

MILLIONAIRE RESOURCE:

Read: Tools of Titans, by Tim Ferriss

CHAPTER 139

Remember Where You Came From

Once you become successful, it's easy to forget where you started, the breaks you got and the people who helped you get there. Unfortunately, this happens all the time. The enemy of greatness is ego because it stifles your growth and alienates those who can help you climb even higher. Arrogance is not attractive, and it's rooted in a lack of emotional discipline. Most of us come from humble beginnings,

and we are well served to remember that as we rise in wealth and stature. As easy as this seems, it's easier to fall victim to continuous praise. In the early stages of this process you feel unworthy, but as you continue to hear it, you begin to believe it. And when anyone challenges the idea that you are as praiseworthy as people say, it's easy to take offense when you're used to seeing yourself in a certain light. The problem with this ego driven state is that the people you meet in this exalted position are already on your side. The people that you need to influence are usually the ones that are not so sure about you, and your anger or frustration towards them may impede your progress. The secret is to stay humble and constantly remind yourself of where you've come from and what it took to get you here. Remember the mistakes you've made and the struggles you've endured along your path to prosperity. This will help you remain unaffected when you're criticized and grateful for the successes you've enjoyed. People are attracted by humility and repelled by hubris. No one wants to help someone who's full of himself. No matter how high you climb and how rich you get, be sure to pepper your response to praise with phrases like "Lucky breaks" Great mentors" and "Right place at the right time." These may or may not be true, but either way, they will endear you to those who may be able to help you rise even higher.

QUOTE:

"It is always the secure who are humble."—G.K. Chesterton

ACTION STEP:

Notice how people are attracted to authentic humility and repelled by authentic hubris.

CRITICAL THINKING QUESTION:

How can being humble help you get ahead?

MILLIONAIRE RESOURCE:

Read: The Self-Esteem Workbook for Teens, by Lisa Schab

CHAPTER 140

Be Nice

Your future wealth and success will place you in a position of power. There's an old saying: "Absolute power corrupts absolutely." Don't let this happen to you. Refuse to allow yourself to abuse the power that your status in the world provides you. Be nice to people. Be good to them. Not because you have to; but because it's the right thing to do. Treat people as you wish for them to treat you, and maybe even a little better. There are two kinds of powerful people in the world: the ego driven upper class, and the spirit driven world class. The former is self-absorbed and abusive, and the latter is self-aware and inclusive. The upper-class performer thinks only of the bottom line; the net result and the profit he can achieve. The world-class performer is guided by his inner spirit, and he values matters of the heart. One is a cold-blooded, win at all costs machine and the other is a high functioning, emotionally well-adjusted human being. The enemy of the spirit is ego, and the enemy of ego is spirit. Being a self-made millionaire doesn't give you the right to be mean or indifferent. As a matter of fact, your position power should create an inner sense of gratitude for your good fortune that leads you to be as nice, encouraging and uplifting to others. You will see others using their powers to hurt people and bolster their feelings of self-importance. The world is full of successful jerks, and the best thing you can do is to not become one of them. So be nice and go out of your way to help, inspire and motivate others to be their best and feel their best. You're one of the luckiest people in the world, and the least you can do as payback for your good fortune is to be nice to people who don't have the power to help or hurt you.

QUOTE:

"You're never too important to be nice to people."—Jon Batiste

ACTION STEP:

Go out of your way this week to be nice to someone you don't like.

CRITICAL THINKING QUESTION:

Do you believe that the more successful you become, the nicer you should be?

MILLIONAIRE RESOURCE:

Read: Everyday Leadership: Attitude and Actions for Respect and Success, by Mariam G. MacGregor (A guidebook for teens)

CHAPTER 141

Be at Peace with Yourself

As you get older, you'll hear people talk about the importance of peace of mind. This is the calm, easy feeling that everything is ok. The mistake many middle-class thinkers make with peace of mind is that they see it as something that's created outside of themselves. This is a mistake. Peace of mind is a gift you give yourself. It is not created through circumstances but by the decision of the beholder. The secret of this self-induced state of mind is to be at peace with yourself. In other words, only speak and act in ways that make you feel good about yourself. Avoid any behavior that threatens your inner peace. Always do your best, and that will give leave you with a peaceful feeling even when you lose. Everyone makes mistakes, and you will, too. The key is learning to forgive and make peace with yourself. You must be your own best friend, and that means letting go of any self-doubts, fears or even hatred you may be harboring. Avoid doing things that risk the reputation you have with yourself, and never act in a manner that breaches your integrity or your values. Tell yourself that no matter what happens in your life, you can handle it. This will give you peace of mind that most people only dream of. Many people are afraid that they won't be able to handle the major crises of their lives. The truth is they are much tougher and more resilient than they think, yet they suffer needlessly worrying about a crisis that may never happen. Don't fall into this emotional trap. Know that you are tough enough to handle anything life throws at you and enjoy the peace that accompanies that belief.

QUOTE:

"Set peace of mind as your highest goal, and organize your life around it."—Brian Tracy

ACTION STEP:

What are three things you can do every day that will give you more peace of mind?

CRITICAL THINKING QUESTION:

Who in your life seems to have the most peace of mind?

MILLIONAIRE RESOURCE:

Read: Peace of Mind: Insights on Human Nature that Can Change Your Life, by Joshua L. Liebman

CHAPTER 142

Consciousness is Contagious

The way you think, speak and behave will have an impact on the people around you. Others will have the same influence on you. Consciousness, or thinking, is contagious. You'll tend to act like those in your inner circle, and they will tend to act like you. The implications of this phenomenon are substantial because your success, fulfillment, and happiness will be directly impacted by the people in which you spend the most time. This means you must choose your inner circle carefully and strategically. Surround yourself with three different people: people that are more successful; people who are supportive and people you love. The more successful people will push you to reach higher and expect more from yourself. They will make you think bigger, work harder and expand your vision. The supportive people will serve as a positive influence in your life and business. And the people who love you will be there to cheer you on in victory and console you in defeat. They love you for who you are, not what you have. This group will become your most valuable asset over time because they want nothing from you outside of your friendship and love. These people will become your most trusted advisors; people who will always serve your best interests. People that have a negative attitude; those that think small and act smaller, and others who weaken your resolve, drain your energy or break your spirit are to be avoided like the plaque. Either cut them out of your life or limit the time you spend with them. Their consciousness is as contagious as chicken pox, and they pose a serious threat to your success, especially in the early years as you are climbing. Guard your mind as intensely as you guard your money, and it will continue to expand and grow.

QUOTE:

"People inspire you, or they drain you. Pick them wisely."—Hans Hansen

ACTION STEP:

Make a new friend in school that you think would have a positive influence on you.

CRITICAL THINKING QUESTION:

Are most of your friends better students than you?

MILLIONAIRE RESOURCE:

Read: Social Rules for Kids: The Top 100 Social Rules Kids Need to Succeed, by Susan Diamond, M.A.

CHAPTER 143

Seek Fulfillment

Make no mistake: money and success are important. Anyone who denies this is either delusional or foolish. Most people spend the majority of their waking hours worried or thinking about how they're going to pay for the things they want in life. That's why the information in this book will serve you well. Your best strategy is to find something you love to do, that serves people and make your fortune doing it. That's the ultimate formula for success. Some people simply seek wealth at any cost, doing anything that creates it, but this strategy will rob you of the emotional fulfillment that accompanies succeeding at something you truly enjoy and wholeheartedly believe in. There's nothing that matches the emotional high of spending your days providing a product or service that you would gladly provide for free. When you're in this position, the real joy comes not from the money, but from the act of doing something you love to do. If you simply seek riches, you may miss fulfillment. If you seek fulfillment, you will feel good and be happy in the process of pursuing wealth. When you're doing something you love to do, the only reward you need is the experience of doing it. That's why some people spend their entire lives chasing their passions. This is a great start, but it's only half of an intelligent strategy. The other half is finding a way to make a fortune while basking in the beauty of a fulfilling occupation. Granted, this is not an easy combination to create, but it is a worthy goal. This equation is no match for someone like you, who is a master of sustained effort and concentration. While your friends are goofing off, you should be discovering your passion and thinking about how to turn it into a fortune.

QUOTE:

"Success without fulfillment is the ultimate failure."—Tony Robbins

ACTION STEP:

Write down the three activities that give you the most fulfillment.

CRITICAL THINKING QUESTION:

Do you believe it's possible to become rich and fulfilled at the same time?

MILLIONAIRE RESOURCE:

Read: What Color is Your Parachute for Teens, by Carol Christen and Richard N. Bolles

CHAPTER 144

Use Laughter

As you embark on your journey to become a self-made millionaire, you'll want to employ some nonlinear strategies to help make the process easier and more enjoyable. Using laughter to reduce the stress and intensity of striving for success is one of the most overlooked, underused techniques. Of course, people love to laugh, and we all engage in it when something strikes us as funny. That's fine, but I'm not talking about that. What I'm suggesting is that you use laughter as an active strategy, not merely a passive response. The reason is simple: the more you laugh, the looser you become. It's hard to be creative and solve tough problems when you're wound up tight. Laughter lightens the load and brings joy to your daily activities. And it doesn't have to be the kind of laughter that makes you roll on the floor. Little laughs, many times per day is better than one big laugh. Search for things that generate humor, whether they're cartoons, clips from funny movies or stories. Humor is everywhere, and the source in which you find it isn't nearly as important as how it makes you feel. Laughing will add fun to the days that would otherwise not be enjoyable, and it will make your good days even better. Possibly the best place to find humor is by looking at yourself and some of the quirky things you do. Whether it's shampooing your hair in the shower, and 5 minutes later forgetting if you did it or not, or it's some of the conversations you have with yourself. Laughing at yourself is among of the healthiest habits you can adopt, and when you share your humorous idiosyncrasies with others, it endears them to you. There's something attractive about a person who can laugh and make fun of themselves. As simple as it seems, building this habit is a world-class strategy that few people understand and even fewer employ.

QUOTE:

"There is little success where there is little laughter."—Andrew Carnegie

ACTION STEP:

Learn how to make other people laugh.

CRITICAL THINKING QUESTION:

Can you learn to think funny?

MILLIONAIRE RESOURCE:

Read: Crazy-Stressed: Saving Today's Overwhelmed Teens with Love, Laughter and the Science of Resilience, by Michael J. Bradley

CHAPTER 145

Pursue Power

Becoming a self-made millionaire will give you power. Power to make your own decisions, to pursue your passions and to live life on your own terms.

While money is the primary source of power, things such as where you received your education, where you live, the clubs you belong to and the people you associate with, are also important. The world is not a level playing field. It would be nice if it were. It would be fairer, but it's not. Even in a free market economy, like America, where everyone has the same opportunity to succeed, it's still not as easy to make it for some as it is for others. Some of the differences are intelligence, ambition, and focus. These are typically assets people are born or not born with. But what I'm referring to are the savvy strategies of the rich and successful; strategies that give them power. Power has a bad reputation because some people abuse it, but power used ethically is a wonderful thing. Beware of the middle-classes beliefs around people who pursue power: they are not good. Most people view power as a negative thing, and they believe that the people who pursue it are evil, greedy and mean. Never let the average person's limited beliefs negatively affect your own. The first step in your pursuit of power should be your grades in school. The better you do in school, the more power you have with teachers and others in the academic community. Outstanding grades will give you the opportunity to create the next power play, which is being accepted into a world-class University. A community college will give you a good education, but it doesn't offer you the power of attending Harvard, Yale or Stanford. The powerful people you connect with at a world-class University will add to your own power. After school, building a successful business or career, living in the right neighborhood and belonging to the right country club will allow mixing with people of major influence, which will make you even more powerful. My last suggestion on pursuing power is to do it quietly and carefully. Don't broadcast this strategy lest you be labeled a 'social climber,' which is someone seeking status through associations. Your goal is *true power*, not status, but to many people, the process appears the same. Be smart and calculated in your approach to minimize any negative effects of this strategy.

QUOTE:

"The measure of a man is what he does with power." —Plato

ACTION STEP:

Consider running for school council or some other powerful position.

CRITICAL THINKING QUESTION:

Who are the most powerful kids in school, and why?

MILLIONAIRE RESOURCE:

Read: How to Win at College, by Cal Newport

CHAPTER 146

Share Credit

You're going to be a world-class success. There's no question about it. You have everything you need to become as rich and successful as you wish. But to build an empire, you're going to need help. Fulfilling your vision will take a team of smart and dedicated people. You will end up spending the majority of your time and with these people, and they will display their loyalty by always serving your best interests. They will work for you, support you and fight for you. This team of champions will watch your back and protect you from those who would take advantage. In exchange for their brainpower, dedication, and loyalty, you will pay them premium compensation and offer them every opportunity. The most you can do for them has nothing to do with money, profit sharing or perks. It's an emotional reward that they deserve that many leaders refuse to give, and that's sharing the credit for your success. This is not a gift or generous display of humility. The credit you share will be credit they have *earned.* No matter how many people praise you and call you brilliant, you wouldn't have succeeded without your team. The quarterback may throw the game-winning pass, but without the offensive line, he'd be on the ground before he ever wound up. Make credit sharing a priority in your business, and teach your leaders to do the same. Be sure to share credit publicly, not just privately. Sharing credit in public amplifies its impact, and it will make your team feel good about themselves, your company, and you as their leader. Never let the outside world convince you that you are the sole factor in your success, because no matter how smart you are, large-scale success is a team sport. Don't allow your ego to interfere with reality, and your team will appreciate the acknowledgment.

QUOTE:

"A good leader takes a little more than his share of the blame, a little less than his share of the credit."—Arnold H. Glasgow

ACTION STEP:

Share credit with someone today.

CRITICAL THINKING QUESTION:

How often do you share credit for your successes?

MILLIONAIRE RESOURCE:

Read: Teen Leadership Revolution: How Ordinary Teens Become Extraordinary Leaders, by Tom Thelen

CHAPTER 147

Have Fun

You're going to have to work hard for what you want. Long hours, lost sleep and self-sacrifice all are part of achieving world-class success. While your friends in school are goofing off and getting into trouble, trying to do as little as possible to pass, you will be giving your school work everything you have. This is not easy. Many of your classmates will ridicule you. The secret is to stay focused and on track towards your goals. The more you enjoy your success, the easier it is to keep working toward your next victory. Now I'm not referring to the fun that most people have. Cutting up in class, seeing how much you can get away with, and flirting with classmates is how most students have fun. What I'm talking about is enjoying the fun that comes from getting what you want. Getting A's on tests, being recognized by your teachers for outstanding work and winning a seat on the student council is the kind of fun you should pursue. Succeeding in areas that will help you build the life you desire is the goal. Now, this doesn't mean you can't be frivolous from time to time and simply enjoy the fun of being your age. This is healthy. What I'm suggesting is that most of the time you should be more focused on the fun of success than the fun of frivolity. It not only creates a deeper sense of joy, but it moves you closer towards your goals. Learning to equate success with fun is a formidable habit you want to develop because it will stay with you for the rest of your life. The masses associate fun with minimal effort and maximum pleasure; which is why everyone thinks the class clown is cool. In reality, the class clown rarely succeeds. It's the quiet kid in the corner of the class that usually excels in school and life. Follow the path of the great performers, and have fun winning and getting what you want.

QUOTE:

"People rarely succeed unless they have fun in what they are doing."
—Dale Carnegie

ACTION STEP:

Have fun succeeding at something today.

CRITICAL THINKING QUESTION:

What's the most fun job you can imagine?

MILLIONAIRE RESOURCE:

Read: Mindful Games: Sharing Mindfulness and Meditation for Children, Teens and Families, by Susan Kaiser Greenland

CHAPTER 148

Set Your Own Benchmarks

Success is a funny thing. When you're striving for it, no one seems to notice. When you achieve it, *everyone* seems to notice. You move from being invisible to being a hero. The second most surprising part is if you lose it or experience a series of setbacks, you'll begin to feel invisible again. If you understand how the world treats success and failure, none of this is a problem. If you don't, then you're likely to find yourself on an emotional roller coaster, forever contemplating the significance or insignificance of your existence. If you gauge your success by how the world reacts to the ebb and flow of your results, you place your own sense of fulfillment and happiness in their hands. This is a mistake. A better strategy is to set your own milestones and benchmarks and keep your own score. You will have failures that feel like victories, and successes that feel like failures. Winning can be an odd experience, and you want to maintain a level head no matter what the outside world is saying. Over thousands of years that man has been walking upright and thinking for himself, society has agreed upon the various criteria of success. Don't allow these to set the bar for you. Set your own goals, and dream your own dreams, regardless of what people say. Create your own expectations and fulfill your own potential. And if society makes you a hero for your achievements, so be it. If not, don't waste a minute worrying about it. The odds are that at certain periods in your life you will be recognized, and maybe even idolized, by some people in society. But with big dreams come big risks, and sometimes those risks go the wrong way. That's when the people that once worshipped you will now ignore you. This is why it's critical to keep your own counsel and decide on what success means to you. Set your goals and your benchmarks to track your progress and ignore what society say's is success or failure. This will keep you in control of your own, emotions, peace of mind and happiness.

QUOTE:

"If you want to be a successful person, set your own benchmarks, achieve them, break them and repeat that cycle until you are not satisfied." —Shubham Tiwari

ACTION STEP:

Write down your first success benchmark in school for the next 90 days and begin moving toward it.

CRITICAL THINKING QUESTION:

What benchmarks have you used with success in the past?

MILLIONAIRE RESOURCE:

Read: Are My Kids on Track?, by Sissy Goff, David Thomas, and Melissa Trevathan

CHAPTER 149

Be Humble

People love to worship heroes. We love our sports legends, movie stars, and business tycoons. Society turns these people into Gods, and that kind of treatment can turn a well-adjusted person into an egomaniac. This is why it's critical that no matter how much praise and positive attention you get, that you remain humble. At times you will feel undeserving of the accolades, and at other times you will feel like you deserve more. Never let the outside world determine your inner world, or how you act towards yourself and others. Confidence is attractive, arrogance is not. If you remain humble, people will rally around you during tough times and celebrate with you during good times. Humility is magnetic. It makes people feel good about you and motivates them to help, support and promote you. The enemy of humility is ego, and no one wants to associate with people that have an excessive amount of it. As easy as it sounds to avoid getting caught up in your own self-importance, the truth is that it's not. When everyone around you is praising every move you make, it's easy to be offended when others don't. You begin to believe you deserve special treatment because you've done special things. You don't, but sometimes it's hard to see it. The fastest way to move your mind from an ego-based consciousness to a spirit-based consciousness is to remember where you came from and be grateful to everyone who helped you get where you are. Gratitude and hubris cannot coexist, so channeling your feelings from self-love to gratitude is a great strategy to keep your mind in check and your career moving forward. Start each day by writing down 5 things that you're grateful for, and you'll build the foundation for a happy life full of success, fun, and friendships.

QUOTE:

"Pride makes us artificial and humility makes us real." —Thomas Merton

ACTION STEP:

Just for today, add more humility to your general discourse.

CRITICAL THINKING QUESTION:

On a scale of 1-7, 7 being most humble, how humble are you?

MILLIONAIRE RESOURCE:

Read: Humility: An Unlikely Biography of America's Greatest Virtue, by David J. Bobb

CHAPTER 150

Know the Power of Persistence

You are expecting greatness in your life. Tremendous grades in school, acceptance into a world-class College or University, pursuing a career you love surrounded by people who love you. This is the good life. Along the way, there may be stumbling blocks and setbacks. At times, it may seem as though you have it all figured out, and then suddenly, it will all fall apart. At your darkest times, when it seems hopeless, luck will suddenly favor you, and the darkness will clear. This predictable pattern has nothing to do with you or success. It's just the way life works. This is why you must understand and embrace the pure power of persistence. The tireless pursuit of a worthy goal has been responsible for every great achievement of mankind. Overnight successes happen, but mostly in movies. In the real world, winning takes time. The masters of success are people who refuse to be denied the vision they hold in their heart. No matter how many times they fail, they always get back on their feet. Very few problems and obstacles can sustain the consistent, persistent, laser-focus of a problem solver that refuses to quit. During this process, there will be times when you are frustrated, exhausted and weary from your efforts and failed attempts. This is when the average person stops, and the extraordinary person starts. For the super-achiever, the process doesn't even get interesting until this point, where the problem proves itself worthy of his intellect. This is when middle- class performers fold, and world-class performers shine. Even at the point of despair, they keep moving forward. Once the problem is solved, society labels the performer a genius, but the truth is that genius rarely has anything to do with it. *Persistence* is the real star of the show. This is another reason that you must select work that you love. That way, when you're fighting your way to the top, you will know that it's worth it.

QUOTE:

"Ambition is the path to success. Persistence is the vehicle you arrive in."—Bill Bradley

ACTION STEP:

Apply persistence to an area of your life in which you care about succeeding.

CRITICAL THINKING QUESTION:

In which area of your life have you been the most persistent?

MILLIONAIRE RESOURCE:

Read: The Dip: A Little Book That Teaches You When to Quit, and When To Stick, by Seth Godin

CHAPTER 151

Exercise

Physical exercise has so many benefits that it's difficult to overstate its impact on a person's life. The type of exercise you choose is almost irrelevant, as long as you choose some way to keep your body moving. Besides keeping your body weight under control and the physical benefits gained from exercise, there are multiple psychological benefits. Feelings of optimism, good humor, and overall well-being are associated with physical activity. These benefits will serve you in almost every aspect of your life, and the older you get, the more important they will become. Right now you're young, and exercise is easy. This is a good thing. The best strategy is to try as many sports and other physical activities as you can to see which ones you love to play. The idea is to select a sport you love and can play forever, like tennis and golf. Give weight training a try as well, because studies have shown that maintaining and building muscle mass is a key factor in staying fit and healthy. You don't have to become a body builder or competitive athlete to reap the rewards of exercise. As a matter of fact, moderate exercise is usually healthier and safer. The more extreme the sport or activity, the greater the risk of injury. The key is selecting something you enjoy so you will stick to it. Consistent physical activity will help keep you mentally sharp and emotionally resilient, and that will lead to better ideas, clearer thinking, and less stress. There are no magic formulas to success in life, but exercise is close as it gets. The wide range of benefits is so vast that this strategy should not be overlooked.

QUOTE:

"The purpose of training is to tighten the slack, toughen the body, and polish the spirit."—Morihei Ueshiba

ACTION STEP:

Try tennis and golf.

CRITICAL THINKING QUESTION:

How many hours per week do you exercise?

MILLIONAIRE RESOURCE:

Read: The Inner Game of Tennis, by Tim Gallwey

CHAPTER 152

Embrace Fear

Fear is part of the human condition. And while no one enjoys being scared, there are benefits to using the energy it generates. When you're afraid of not doing well on a test, you study. When you're worried that your Mom might withhold your weekly allowance, you work. When you're fearful that you won't have enough money to go to college, you save. Make no mistake: fear isn't fun. It will stress you out, keep you up and ruin a good day. But as a person being groomed for greatness, your job is to eliminate, transcend, or harness your fear to serve your best interests. Like any powerful emotion, the foundation of fear is energy, and it can be directed and manipulated. Positive energy is healthier and more fun, and that's why your first strategy is to eliminate or transcend fear. But if you can't shake it, the next best thing is to harness the fear-based energy you feel and direct it like a laser toward the most productive activity that will eventually eliminate it. An example would be worrying about money, which is a common fear, especially among the masses. Instead of sitting around suffering, turn the fear into the most effective action that will lead to its dilution or elimination. Apply for a job; start a business or create a new budget or savings plan. As soon as you begin to take action, you will feel the fear begin to subside, and this will put you in control of your emotions. No one looks forward to feeling fearful, but no matter how high you rise in life, you will experience it. Refuse to ignore it or run from it. Instead, look it straight in the eyes, acknowledge and embrace it. Then take immediate and bold action to destroy and replace it with feelings of empowerment and positivity.

QUOTE:

"Everything you want is on the other side of fear." —Jack Canfield

ACTION STEP:

In the next seven days, do something you're afraid to do.

CRITICAL THINKING QUESTION:

If you were fearless, what is the first thing you would do?

MILLIONAIRE RESOURCE:

Read: FEAR: Essential Wisdom for Getting Through The Storm, by Thich Nhat Hanh

CHAPTER 153

Life Isn't Fair

Despite your teachers, coaches, clergy and other adults of influence trying to persuade you of the fact that life is fair, the good guys always win, and the bad guys always lose, don't believe it. It's wishful thinking at best and self-delusion at worst. The masses operate from a fear-based consciousness, which makes them prone to making leaps in logic that defy critical thinking. Ignorance scares them, so they often attempt to explain the unexplainable through magical means. A common belief held by the masses is that everything happens for a reason, which comforts them during times of crisis. This belief is an emotional opiate the masses use to quell their fears and to make sense of the random nature of life. Replace this delusional thinking with the belief that no matter what happens in your life, you have the mental toughness, tenacity, and perseverance to survive and thrive in it. Remember that as smart and educated as your teachers, coaches and parents friends are, they are emotional creatures subject to frighteningly high levels of psychological delusion. Is there a reason that every seven seconds, somewhere in the world, a child starves to death? Is there a reason a family is having dinner in a restaurant and is savagely gunned down by a religious terrorist? As unnerving as it can be to human beings, life is unfair and events, both positive and negative, are random. This is the harsh reality of life, and the faster you embrace it, the more successful you will be. The only delusional thinkers that get rich are the ones that sell delusion to the naïve masses who are starving to believe anything that eases their fears. The closer to objective reality that you operate, the richer you will become and the happier you will be. Disneyland is a wonderful place to visit, but you don't want to live there. Let the masses live with Peter Pan in Never Land while you're toughening up to the real world and learning how to navigate it successfully.

QUOTE:

"Life isn't fair, and success isn't free. Welcome to the jungle." —Mental Toughness University marketing slogan.

ACTION STEP:

"For kids ages 15 and above, read the novel Atlas Shrugged, by Ayn Rand, with your parents. This is known as "The book of billionaires."

CRITICAL THINKING QUESTION:

How many of your most closely-held beliefs about life can be proven through evidence?

MILLIONAIRE RESOURCE:

Study several YouTube videos on novelist/philosopher Ayn Rand.

CHAPTER 154

Consider Philanthropy

As a self-made millionaire living and working in a free society, you have the right to spend and invest your fortune in any manner you choose. You can travel the world; indulge in exotic pleasures, build a mansion or anything else your heart desires. Wealth gives you choices, and in the 21st century, those choices are almost endless. As someone who has experienced wealth, I can tell you it's fun to have nice things. Multiple homes, fast cars and every toy you can imagine are only one phone call away. But you may also want to consider the idea of giving back to people, or causes, that are close to your heart. Giving can be one of the most fulfilling experiences you'll ever have. I'm not suggesting that you're obligated to give, or that because you are rich, that you somehow owe it to others. You don't. You earned your money by solving problems people were willing to pay for. It's that simple. Never let the masses persuade you that you are your brother's keeper. *You are not.* I'm not saying you shouldn't help others and share your wealth; only that you shouldn't feel *guilty* if you decide not to. Philanthropy is most fulfilling when it's a conscious choice you make, and you're not looking for anything in return. It's a wonderful feeling to be inspired to help someone in need that sincerely appreciates it. No house you'll ever own or car you'll ever drive will replace the feeling of emotional satisfaction you'll experience when you see the look of relief and gratitude in the eyes of someone you invested time or money in. It's a look you'll never forget, and it may further pull you into the world of philanthropy. You may or may not enjoy this luxury of wealth, but I suggest that when you get rich, you try it once and see how it makes you feel. Choose your beneficiary carefully, and offer your gift in person so you can feel their energy when they accept it. If it grabs you emotionally, make it part of your life. If it doesn't, find a different way to enjoy your success.

QUOTE:

"I've learned that you shouldn't go through life with a catchers mitt on both hands; you need to be able to throw something back."—Maya Angelou

ACTION STEP:

In the next thirty days, find a way to give something to someone in need, with no expectation of getting anything in return, and see how it makes you feel.

CRITICAL THINKING QUESTION:

Does philanthropy have the power to add to your happiness in life?

MILLIONAIRE RESOURCE:

Read: The Givers: Wealth, Power and Philanthropy in a New Gilded Age, by David Callahan

CHAPTER 155

Embrace Love

This book was designed to groom you for high-level financial and life success, and I hope it's succeeded. Anyone who tells you being rich and successful is overrated, has never been rich and successful. To the contrary, being rich and successful is *underrated*. The ability to live life on your own terms, in your own way, is beyond amazing. It's a dream. A fantasy. And I want you to experience every aspect of it. But I would be remiss if I didn't mention the role that love will play in your personal and professional evolution. Not just the love of what you do, who you are or how you spend your days; but also the *love of people*. Especially the people you care about most. You can live in the grandest mansion, drive the fastest car and have the hottest girl or boyfriend on your arm, but without the people you love most in your life, none of these things will matter. It's fun to live in a mansion unless you're alone staring at the walls. It's a rush parading around town in a red Ferrari unless you have no friends or family in which to share it. Travel is wonderful unless you have no one to show your vacation photos. The world is littered with millionaires that undervalued love and personal relationships as they were amassing their fortunes, and they are now among the loneliest people. As wonderful as money is, it's not enough to live a world-class life, or what philosopher Ayn Rand called an 'unrestricted existence.' The fact is that the *utility value of money is convex*, which means its value is high when you're meeting the basic needs of life, but becomes less valuable as you collect more of it. Care for the people who love you for who you are, *not what you own*. You'll know the imposters; they are the ones who always want something from you. Your true friends won't. They will be there through thick and thin, and they will celebrate your successes and sympathize with your failures. Don't let them slip away as you're busy building your empire.

QUOTE:

"Money can buy you a fine dog, but only love can make him wag his tail."—Kinky Friedman

ACTION STEP:

Make a list of the people you love and tell them how much they mean to you.

CRITICAL THINKING QUESTION:

Are you spending enough time with the people you love?

MILLIONAIRE RESOURCE:

Read: The Love Code, by Alexander Loyd, Ph.D.

CHAPTER 156

Have Integrity

One of the things that separate the world-class from the middle-class is *integrity*. The average person makes promises but only keeps them if they're convenient. They tell people they're going to call them back, help them out or be there when needed, but they rarely follow through on their commitments. Integrity means doing what you say you're going to do, and the masses only do what's comfortable. The world-class is different. These people only make promises and commitments that they can keep. This isn't always easy, but it's essential for anyone who wishes to walk with the great ones. This starts in school. When you tell your parents and teachers that you're going to get good grades, are you true to your word? When you tell them you have put your best effort into your homework assignments, is this really the case? When you claim that you're paying close attention to the teacher in class, are you telling the truth? The problem is it's easy to lie, especially when there's little chance of getting caught. The world-class thinker always does the right thing, and he operates out of complete integrity. If you're going to become a self-made success, *this is what you must do*. People you deal with have to know you will always do everything you say you will do, not matter how inconvenient or painful it may be. This habit places you among a small and select group of people, whom everyone wants to do business with. When people know you have integrity, your handshake becomes an ironclad contract they can count on. This is the foundation of every self-made fortune, and all that's required to make it happen is the decision to operate with integrity.

QUOTE:

"Integrity is not something you show others. It is how you behave behind their back."

ACTION STEP:

Over the next 30 days, notice how many times you keep your promises.

CRITICAL THINKING QUESTION:

On a scale of 1-7, 7 being best, how would you rate your level of integrity?

MILLIONAIRE RESOURCE:

Read: Integrity: The Courage to Meet the Demands of Reality by Dr. Henry Cloud

CHAPTER 157

Believe in Yourself

As a striver and achiever, you will attempt many great things. The odds are that some will be successful, and others won't. The road to world-class success is usually paved with setbacks, disappointments, and failures. These are the building blocks that eventually create major successes. Along this journey, you will have the counsel of many, but you will only have to answer to one: yourself. After everyone has weighed in with their opinions and offered their advice, you will be left alone to determine your own destiny. Some of your closest friends, mentors, and advisors may disagree and even break ranks with you. You may be shocked at the behavior of people whom you counted as your closest allies and friends. Some may abandon you, but here's the secret to survival: *never abandon yourself.* In other words, never abandon the belief you have in yourself, your values and ideas. As long as you believe in yourself, there is hope for a better future. Believing in yourself makes you an army of one, and in the end, that will serve as the core of your success. Remember that people follow leaders, and leaders believe in themselves. The certainty of thought and swiftness of action are two hallmarks of strong leaders. In an uncertain world full of fear, the leader who takes bold and decisive action is the leader people follow. This starts right now when you're in school. The goof-offs in your class look up to the kids getting good grades. They may not show it, but they secretly wish they could be a great student like you. Since it's cooler to make heroes out of football stars than it is out of scholars, you may feel like an outcast. This is an error in judgment. Everyone in school secretly admires the kids getting the best grades, although most kids are afraid to show it. The bottom line is that no matter what happens in your life, you must always believe in yourself and your ability to handle whatever life throws at you. You may lose the popular vote, but never allow yourself to lose your own support. We all make mistakes and bad decisions. That's part of life, and the more ambitious you are, the more errors you will make. Learn to accept your failures, mistakes, and bad judgments and move on. Always believe in yourself and your ability to come back, even if everyone else gives up on you.

QUOTE:

"If you don't believe in yourself, no one else will."

ACTION STEP:

Start telling yourself everyday that you believe in yourself and your ability to handle anything that life throws at you.

CRITICAL THINKING QUESTION:

Do you believe in yourself enough to attempt to become one of the best students in your class?

MILLIONAIRE RESOURCE:

Read: How to Become a Straight-A Student, by Cal Newport

CHAPTER 158

Enjoy the Ride

Life goes fast. I know that it doesn't feel like it now, but your perception will change, as you get older. No one knows how long he or she will live, so the smartest strategy is to stay focused on what you want to achieve and move with urgency towards your dreams. This is not the easiest way to live, but if you want to fulfill your potential and live an uncommon life, it's your best shot. There is no guarantee of success, but with your early success education, you have every advantage. The strange thing you'll find about striving for success is that while it seems harder than taking it slow or playing it safe, it's not. The people that subscribe to a lazy lifestyle are often those who don't believe in themselves. Every day is the same recipe of doing the minimal amount of work with the least amount of effort. This seems appealing on the surface, but don't be fooled. Laziness is a formula for losing, boredom, and depression. The achiever's approach to life is exciting, fast paced and pregnant with possibilities. The only downside to aggressively chasing success and financial prosperity is that sometimes the pace becomes so fast, that it's easy to miss significant milestones. The key to avoiding this is to stay grounded and remember from where you came. Slow down enough to celebrate even the smallest victories. This can be tougher than it sounds because when you're moving like a locomotive thundering down the track towards your goals and dreams, it's almost painful to slow down. Slow down anyway, because you'll never be able to go back in time and celebrate. It doesn't have to be for long, but be sure to mark the occasion, for you shall never pass this way again. What I'm trying to say is, enjoy the ride. Successes and failures will come and go. People will come in and out of your life. Things will get better, worse and better again. Life moves in cycles, and it doesn't last forever. So enjoy all of it, even the struggles. If you can do this, you will have pulled off the ultimate victory.

QUOTE:

'Remember, you only have one ride through life, so give it all you got and enjoy the ride." —Jon Gordon

ACTION STEP:

Just for today, consciously enjoy every aspect your day.

CRITICAL THINKING QUESTION:

Are you celebrating your successes, no matter how big or small?

MILLIONAIRE RESOURCE:

Read: The Tao of Teenagers: A Guide to Teen Health, Happiness, Happiness and Empowerment, by Peter Berg, Ed.D.

CHAPTER 159

Never Marry the Party Girl (Or Bad Boy)

Your wealth and success will attract people, especially those of the opposite sex. Sometimes this starts in school when your intelligence and academic success is on display. People are naturally drawn to winners, and that means you're going to have to sort through a lot of suitors. Some will want you for who you are, others for what you have. Your job is to decipher which is which and who is who because the wrong decision can be devastating. The wrong mate can damage your career, hinder your happiness and make your life miserable. On the other hand, the right mate can make the difference between success and failure, fulfillment and emptiness, happiness and despair. In short, selecting your mate is the single most important decision you will ever make for your overall happiness. The right mate will love and support you, no matter how tough it gets. He/she will celebrate with you when you're up and comfort you when you're down. The magnitude of his/her influence cannot be overstated. The biggest mistake the self-made rich make in this area is selecting their mate based on physical appearance and sexual attraction. Men are more likely to fall into this trap, but successful women are just as susceptible. The allure of the handsome bad boy or beautiful party girl has been responsible for some the of worst mate selections in history. There's an old saying that's been passed down for generations: 'never marry the cheerleader.' This is not a literal slight against cheerleaders; it's a metaphor that warns against marrying someone who is all looks and little substance. Make no mistake: the hottest girl or boy in the world is the one who loves you. Looks fade, but love grows. Choose carefully, because your future depends on it.

QUOTE:

"True lovers don't marry someone they can live with, they marry someone they can't live without."

ACTION STEP:

Make a list of five characteristics you look for in a perspective girl or boyfriend.

CRITICAL THINKING QUESTION:

Who would be your ultimate girl or boyfriend and why?

MILLIONAIRE RESOURCE:

Read: Dating Smarts: What Every Teen Needs to Know to Date, Relate, or Wait!, by Amy Lang, MA

CHAPTER 160

Never Say Die

This is my final piece of advice to you; my young, success bound friend, as you begin your journey to the top. Set your sights on what you want, go after it with the ferocity of a jungle tiger, employ the persistence of a Navy SEAL, and *never say die.* No matter how dark it looks or how tough it gets, keep fighting for your dream until you draw your last breath. People may criticize your ambition, doubt your ability and laugh at your vision. Ignore them, move forward and keep getting stronger. The good times will take care of themselves. When you're winning everyone will be your friend. That's fun, and you should enjoy it while it lasts. But always be mentally and emotionally prepared for the tough times, set backs and failures. Refuse to allow anything or anyone to slow you down or stop you from reaching the heights to which you aspire. Even when it seems hopeless, keep placing one foot in front of the other. Sometimes you will gallop toward success, and other times you will crawl, but in the end, the victory is yours. The most dangerous enemy of your own success is you, and you are also its greatest ally. Only you can determine which force will dominate your mind. It's a decision you make and a promise you keep to yourself. Few dreams can withstand the consistent assault and bombardment of a strategic effort. If you fight for your dream as if you are fighting for your life, you are almost assured of its attainment. Embrace the pain of temporary setbacks, endure the criticism of others, and push past the obstacles that threaten to stop you. Never say die isn't a slogan on a bumper sticker: it's a way of life. It's a gift you give yourself. It's a commitment that tells the world that *you exist* and that you won't go away quietly. It's a do or die attitude, and that's a mindset no one wants to compete against.

QUOTE:

"Never, never, never give up."— Winston Churchill

ACTION STEP:

Make a commitment that from now on, when you want something, you will never quit until you get it.

CRITICAL THINKING QUESTION:

Are you willing to fight for your future?

MILLIONAIRE RESOURCE:

Read: Navy SEAL Mental Toughness: A Guide to Developing an Unbeatable Mind, by Chris Lambertsen

If you adopt this last suggestion, it will make all the others possible.

Good luck and Godspeed, my young friend. Whether in this lifetime or in spirit, I will be cheering you on from the sidelines. ☺

LEARNING RESOURCES

- *Secrets Self-Made Millionaires Teach Their Kids Workbook*
  www.secretsworkbook.com
- *How Rich People Think*
  www.HowRichPeopleThinkBook.com
- *177 Mental Toughness Secrets of the World Class*
  www.mentaltoughnesssecrets.com
- *Mental Toughness University*
  www.mentaltoughnessuniversity.com
- *Fat Loser! Coaching Program*
  www.fatloser.com
- *Die Fat or Get Tough*
  www.diefatbook.com
- *Siebold Success Network Online Store*
  www.sieboldnetwork.com
- *Bill Gove Speech Workshop*
  www.speechworkshop.com
- *The Making of a Million Dollar Mind*
  www.milliondollarmind.com
- *Weekly Critical Thinking Questions*
  Mobile Text Reminders
- *Apprentice Program*
  www.speakersapprentice.com
- *Steve Siebold Media Apperances*
  www.SteveOnTV.com

Secrets Self-Made Millionaires Teach Their Kids

FREE WORKBOOK

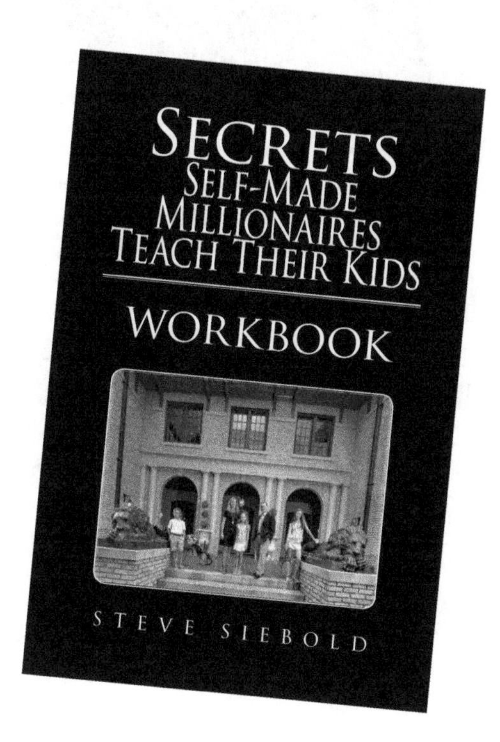

To download FREE workbook please visit:

www.secretsworkbook.com

Mental Toughness University
for Corporate Sales Teams

www.MentalToughnessU.com

MENTAL TOUGHNESS
UNIVERSITY
Are your habits, actions and behaviors congruent with the size and scope of your vision?

HOME TESTIMONIALS CONTACT
Professional Speaker Apprentice Program

MENTAL TOUGHNESS UNIVERSITY
Apprentice
Opportunity
First Name *
Last Name *
Email *
APPLY NOW!

MENTAL TOUGHNESS UNIVERSITY

ABOUT THE AUTHOR

Steve Siebold is an internationally recognized authority in the field of psychological performance training. His clients include Johnson& Johnson, Procter & Gamble, Toyota, GlaxoSmithKline, Caterpillar, and hundreds of others.

Since 1984, Siebold has interviewed over 1,200 self-made millionaires and billionaires, and these interviews continue today. His books, 177 Mental Toughness Secrets of the World Class, and How Rich People Think, are best sellers with over 300,000 copies in print and translated into six languages.

Siebold has been featured on The Today Show, Good Morning America, CNN World News, Fox Business Network, CBS News and hundreds of other television shows throughout the country and around the world.

Siebold is the past Chairman the National Speaker's Associations Million Dollar Speakers Club, and he ranks among the top 1% of professional speakers in the world.

Steve Siebold has been married to Dawn Andrews for 32 years and the couple resides at their historic home/office, Bona Allen Mansion, near Atlanta.

CPSIA information can be obtained
at www.ICGtesting.com
Printed in the USA
LVHW05s0146260718
584996LV00006B/253/P